SpringerBriefs in Geography

More information about this series at http://www.springer.com/series/10050

Aharon Kellerman

Geographic Interpretations of the Internet

Springer

Aharon Kellerman
University of Haifa
Haifa
Israel

ISSN 2211-4165 ISSN 2211-4173 (electronic)
SpringerBriefs in Geography
ISBN 978-3-319-33803-3 ISBN 978-3-319-33804-0 (eBook)
DOI 10.1007/978-3-319-33804-0

Library of Congress Control Number: 2016937386

Printed on acid-free paper

This Springer imprint is published by Springer Nature
The registered company is Springer International Publishing AG Switzerland

Dedicated to my granddaughter Alma-Chaya

Preface

This book constitutes yet another building block in my continuous efforts to contribute to the development, establishment and presentation of the geographical dimensions of the Internet. Back in 2002, in my book *The Internet on Earth: A Geography of Information*, I attempted to draw the geography of the Internet, as part of the wider area of the geography of information, focusing mainly on its revelation in real space. My two following books, devoted to the study of mobility, *Personal Mobilities* (2006) and *Daily Spatial Mobilities* (2012), experimented with the Internet as a type of virtual mobility, operated by people side by side with their mobilities in real space. Finally yet significantly, my last book, *The Internet as Second Action Space* (2014), tackled with the more recent trend of individuals using the Internet as an additional operational space, or even as a replacement, for the 'natural' and veteran physical space.

This rather brief book takes yet another course in my continuous exploration of geographical dimensions of the Internet, this time dealing with the geography of the Internet as cyberspace, in its constitution of a special class of space. We will attempt, in the following chapters, to use concepts and notions, all well-known from their role for the basic analysis of real space, for the understanding and interpretation of the Internet as cyberspace. As such, I trust that this book will add another constructive element for the emerging geographical comprehension of the Internet.

The drive for the analysis proposed and developed in this book, and the carrying out of its writing at this specific point in time, have emerged from my own personal experience as a geographer using the Internet extensively, through computers as well as through smartphones, and for continuously expanding purposes. I have been under a growing impression that when making use of the Internet we are actually involved in a geographical experience, albeit in cyberspace, moving among cyberspatial places, and acting within them. This feeling has been enhanced with the continuously improving graphics of Internet screens, coupled with the speed marvels of broadband communications.

Parts of the book constitute an expansion of my recent *GeoJournal* article, entitled 'Image spaces and the geography of Internet screen-space' (2016). Thus,

Chap. 2 of the book is an expansion of the first sections of that article, whereas parts of Chaps. 3–5 present elaborated discussions of terms and concepts listed briefly in latter sections of that article, with a newly added discussion of co-presence. Chapter 6 follows in part yet another article of mine, devoted to cyberspatial cognition (Kellerman 2007).

Most of the terms and concepts that are presented in this book serve as basic tools for geographical analysis in human geography, and their use for the interpretation of the Internet is our basic objective in this book. Albeit, some of the concepts discussed in the following chapters, notably those of distanciation, co-presence, proximity, and directionality, though being straightforward terms for spatial analysis, have not been developed within geography, and geographers have made little use of them. They have rather emerged in sociology, thus pointing to the growing interest of sociologists in space and in spatial organization in general, and in cyberspace in particular. Sociologists have focused on the exploration of the human significance of these dimensions, notably within the recently emerging interdisciplinary study of mobilities.

The book may appeal to the wider communities of human and economic geographers, and it may be of special interest to those involved in information and Internet geographies. The book may also appeal to geographers interested in the terms, concepts, and methods, developed and used by geographers for their analyses of real space, so that this book may provide them with some insights as for their possible extension for the analysis of cyberspace. The book may further be of special interest and importance to sociologists and media scholars and students, notably for those specializing in information society and information technologies, as well as to those dealing with the interrelationships between societies, on the one hand, and communications technologies and the Internet, on the other.

I acknowledge the permission granted by Springer for the use of my *GeoJournal* (2016) article mentioned before, as well as for Fig. 2.1, another version of which was originally published in that article. I further acknowledge the permission granted by Chitika.com for the use of the data presented in Tables 4.1, 4.2 and in Fig. 4.1. Thanks are due to Kety Gersht (Zefat Academic College) for the drawing of Fig. 2.1, and to Noga Yoselevich (University of Haifa) for the drawing of Fig. 7.1.

As always, I owe a deep gratitude to my wife Michal, for her continuous patience and tolerance for what seems to be my unstoppable involvement in research and writing.

March 2016

Reference

Kellerman, A. (2007). Cyberspace classification and cognition: Information and communications cyberspaces. *Journal of Urban Technology, 14*, 5–32.

Contents

List of Figures

List of Tables

Chapter 1
Introduction: The Internet and Geography

Abstract This, introductory chapter will introduce the thesis of the book, its relevance and importance. It will further elaborate on the literature which has attempted so far to relate to the Internet as a geographical space. The chapter will also treat several Internet-related topics, such as digital gaps, sociality, and the territorial geography of the Internet.

Keywords Internet geography · Geographic terminology · Internet foundations · Digital gaps · Internet social spatiality · Terrestrial geography of the internet

1.1 Book Objectives and Structure

The Internet has turned into an integral element of our daily lives in all of their three current major spheres: home, work, and on the go. The Internet constitutes for contemporary societies a triple space: information space through the Web and its websites; communications space through platforms that facilitate e-mailing, chatting, and calling; and Internet screen space, serving as the interface between the first two spaces and their users. As such, the Internet does not only passively 'inform' its users, but it permits the active performance of informational and communications activities of all kinds by its subscribers. The following chapters will introduce a new perspective for the Internet: veteran spatial concepts and terms, developed originally for the description and analysis of real space, will be portrayed, in an attempt to apply them for a geographic interpretation of the Internet. The discussions in the following chapters may jointly put forward an initial systematic geographic interpretation of the system. Thus, the following discussions may possibly shed a significant light on the Internet as a spatial entity, an entity being both similar and different, as compared to real space.

The approach advanced in the book amounts to an extension of numerous and basic real-space geographical concepts for the cyber spatial Internet. Geographers, as well as scholars from adjacent disciplines, notably sociology, have developed these concepts over the years for the understanding and analysis of terrestrial

A. Kellerman, *Geographic Interpretations of the Internet*,
SpringerBriefs in Geography, DOI 10.1007/978-3-319-33804-0_1

geography, and we will try to extend these concepts for the interpretation and analysis of cyberspace. As such, this book differs from previously published books on the geography of the Internet. It does not constitute a general geography book for the terrestrial geography of the Internet, such as Kellerman (2002). Furthermore, the book does not concentrate on specific approaches developed so far for the study of the Internet, like, for instance, global geographies of the Internet (Warf 2013), the e-society (Loo 2012), and the Internet as second action space (Kellerman 2014). Another approach to the spatial study of the Internet focused on detailed comparisons between cyberspace and real space, as well as on some of the relationships between these two categories of space (Kellerman 2002, 2014; Wang et al. 2003), and we will briefly refer to these relationships at the conclusion of this book (Chap. 7).

The following discussions rather attempt to present numerous dimensions and parameters that have been originally developed for the analysis of real spaces and landscapes, as well as for human actors in them, and argue for their direct or borrowed fitting for the analysis and interpretation of the Internet. We will attempt to apply these parameters and dimensions for interpretations of the Internet in general, or for the analysis of one or some of its metaphorically spatial components: communications platforms, websites, and Internet screen spaces. The following presentations of these parameters are not meant to constitute a set of guidelines for website and Web-screen designers, whose design activities are equivalent to those performed by real space planners. It is rather meant here to put forward some geographical parameters for the analysis of the Internet and its components, in similarity to the spatial analysis of real spaces and some of their specific components, as performed in human geography.

The idea of viewing cyberspace in general as being somehow similar to real space in its very nature, as well as in its experiencing by users, is not new. For instance, 'virtual environments contain much of the essential spatial information that is utilized by people in real environments' (Péruch et al. 2000, p. 115), and 'human behavior in cyberspace bears certain similarities with spatial behavior in the physical world' (Kwan 2001, p. 33). However, some differences between human perceptions of these two spaces still apply, for instance 'what is near in physical space is often far in cyberspace, and vice versa' (Adams 1998, p. 93; see also Pickles 2004, p. 159).

Generally speaking, cyberspace both enables and constraints its users in certain ways, some of which we will discover in the following chapters, as is the case, in different ways, though, for the enabling and constraining of individuals by real space (Adams and Ghose 2003). Cyberspace has not developed apart from real space, since its hardware, as well as its users, are located in real space. Thus, 'cyberspace is hardly immaterial in that it is very much an embodied space' (Dodge 2001, p. 1), and from yet another end, 'information systems redefine and do not eliminate geography', and even more so, 'electronic space is embedded in, and often intertwines with, the physical space and place' (Li et al. 2001, p. 701). Thus, the Internet 'is shaped by, and reflects, the place-routed cultures in which it is produced and consumed' (Holloway and Valentine 2001, p. 153). Still, however, the Internet constitutes a 'different human experience of dwelling in the world; new articulations of near and far, present and absent, body and technology, self and environment' (Crang et al. 1999, p. 1). Thus, cyberspace has its own geography, it is symbol-sustained (Benedikt 1991, pp. 123, 191; Batty 1997), and has its own materiality (Kinsley 2014).

Side by side with the specific identity of cyberspace, the very experiencing of the Web (the common short name for the World Wide Web (WWW)), involves a strong imprint of real space: 'space isn't a mere metaphor. The rhetoric and semantics of the Web are those of space. More important, our *experience* of the Web is fundamentally spatial' (Weinberger 2002, p. 35). The elaborations in the following chapters intend to move this wealth of rather general, overall and conceptual statements on cyberspace one-step further, by presenting a list of real space parameters that can be harnessed specifically for the analysis of the Internet and its three spaces (information, communications, and screens).

The following chapters will outline geographical terms grouped into five wide-ranging concepts, which we will attempt to extend for the Internet in the following chapters: space (Chap. 2), structure (Chap. 3), distance (Chap. 4), mobility (Chap. 5), and cognition (Chap. 6). Each of these major concepts serves as a kind of an 'umbrella concept' for several other terms and concepts, as outlined in the book contents, and as discussed in detail in the following chapters. This list of geographical concepts and terms, originally developed and used for the interpretation of real space, is not exclusive, but it rather includes those existing spatial concepts and terms, which seem fit for potential extension and application to the cyber spatial Internet.

One most basic geographical concept, location, will not receive a distinct attention in the discussions in the following chapters, and this is so because location seems to be mostly irrelevant for Internet cyber spatial information and communications spaces. As we will see in Chap. 3, location used to be important in the early years of the Internet, as expressed in preferences by companies and organizations for their domain names. However, location will be shown to be still of importance, though, in our interpretation of distance decay patterns regarding information presented on Internet screen spaces, in Chap. 4. The concept of co-presence, to be presented in Chap. 5, may also mean, in some way, at least, the co-location of individuals using the Internet, simultaneously in both real and virtual spaces.

By the very application of well-known concepts developed originally within traditional human geography for the interpretation of the Internet, the book proposes, and if only a posteriori, some possible transcendence of terminology from real space to cyberspace. This transcendence may further point to some possible combination between terrestrial and virtual geographies, a combination that may help in coping with Internet structures and contents. We will explore this latter question of possible unity or separation between real and virtual spaces, in light of the proposed detailed analyses of the Internet through geographical concepts, in the concluding chapter (Chap. 7) of the book.

The intellectual exercise developed in the following chapters is of significance for geographers, as well as for other students of space, since 'cyberspace itself is deeply structured geographically' (Warf 2006, p. xxvii), and since it may make it easier for students and scholars interested in geography, to interpret the Internet via their veteran and *terra cognita* terminology. In its routine uses by nonprofessionals, the Internet has received some geographical interpretations right from its inception, through the application of several spatial terms for its operation, such as 'website', 'homepage', and 'surfing'. Eventually, the provision of geographic interpretations of the Internet, offered in the following chapters through basic geographical terminology, may serve as an infrastructure for future geographical examinations of the Internet through the application of some more advanced geographical concepts, tools and theories.

In the rest of this chapter, we will discuss some basics for the study of the Internet. Thus, we will begin with the presentation of existing approaches to the geography of the Internet, followed by a short exploration of the origins of the geographical terminology used in this book. We will then continue with the laying down of some of the foundations of the Internet, relating notably to Internet founders, its emergence and diffusion, as well as its early adopters. This discussion will be followed by some comments on Internet public policies, as well as by an exposition of digital gaps in its adoption and use at several geographical scales (global and national), as well as at some social ones (gender and age). Finally, we will explore the social Internet spatiality via its interpretation as social space, followed by a brief exposition of the terrestrial geography of the Internet.

1.2 Approaches to the Geography of the Internet

The notion of geography (or geographies) of virtual spaces, which has been widely studied in recent years, has emerged as a rather vague concept, thus lacking clear and systematic methodologies for its analysis and interpretation. This lack of clear and strictly defined concepts and methodologies is most striking with regard to the rather veteran notion of 'geography of cyberspace', which has emerged as a multifaceted concept. Hence, the geography of cyberspace may refer, first, to the locational dimensions in real space of the hardware, software, cables, and antennas of the Internet, all of which facilitate its very operation in particular, as well as that of telecommunications in general (see e.g. Cai et al. 1999; and the following Sect. 1.6).

The geography of cyberspace may further relate to data at numerous geographical scales (i.e. for cities, regions, and countries), presenting the rates of adoption and use of the Internet, mobile phones, and other communications media and technologies (see e.g. Dodge 1999; and the following Sect. 1.4). At yet a third level, the geography of cyberspace may focus on the geography of the Internet as experienced by its individual users (see Kellerman 2007; Chap. 6). This latter option for the geography of cyberspace relates also to the visible interface of the Internet with its users in form of web pages displayed on computer/smart phone screens, and these screens can be interpreted as spatial units. Fourth, the geography of cyberspace may further consist of the geographical aspects of websites and communications platforms, for instance their location *vis-à-vis* their hosting servers, and the routes of information transmission between them and their users (see e.g. Avidan and Kellerman 2004). The two latter options will be elaborated on in the following Chaps. 2–5.

A recent review of virtual geographies (Kinsley 2014) argued for some fading of the study of cyberspace geography, being replaced by numerous other directions of study. Examples for these new directions of study for virtual geographies are, the study of computer operated, monitored and controlled space, 'code/space' (see e.g. Kitchin and Dodge 2011), or the study of the growing human interaction with computer screens through their touching (e.g. Paterson 2006). A third, and rather novel direction, is the proposed study of 'technicity' 'defined as the qualities of the constitutive relations between the human and the technical' (Kinsley 2014, p. 376).

We believe that the possible fading of the study of cyberspace geography is too early, since some of its basic building blocks still need to be added to the geographical understanding of the virtual and cyber spatial worlds, notably for the Internet. As we mentioned already, the Internet consists of three interrelated spaces: information, communications, and screens. These three spaces will be presented in some detail in the next chapter, and their geographical aspects will be highlighted along the following chapters (Chaps. 3–6).

As we mentioned already, the following discussions of the geographical aspects of the Internet are based on epistemological notions and terms that have been developed along the years for the interpretation of real human-made space and its uses. Interestingly enough, shortly after the emergence of the Internet, Couclelis (probably 1997) proposed this very direction for the study of the geography of the Internet, through her presentation of questions needing answers and development. These questions have not, as of yet, been systematically treated, and hence our attempt to do so in this book. Our discussions of the several geographical terms and concepts for Internet analysis in the following chapters will not be accompanied by empirical testing, since, by their very nature, they present a wide array of notions and terms that permit widely ranging potential empirical applications. Furthermore, it may turn out difficult to apply all of the proposed terms and concepts to the analysis of a single website.

1.3 Geographical Terminology and the Internet

Scholars in most disciplines tend to develop terminology and concepts, in order for them to be used and applied widely for the description, explanation, analysis, assessment and integration of phenomena, patterns and processes. This tendency obviously applies also to human geography. Thus, Earle et al. (1996) differentiated between substantive and methodological concepts in geography. The terms and concepts discussed in the following chapters are clearly substantive ones. Methodological concepts in geography are, for instance, cartographic or statistical terms and concepts, but Earle et al. (1996) preferred to consider as methodological concepts the several epistemologies that have developed within modern human geography, such as the spatial, the humanist and the Marxist ones. The specific substantive concepts and terms introduced in the following chapters for the interpretation of cyberspace were developed and introduced through all the major epistemologies that have emerged in geographical research in the second half of the twentieth century, as well as through the more recent interdisciplinary study of mobility.

More particularly, all of the concepts and terms introduced in Chap. 3 for geographical structures in the Internet, namely ground, place, regions, and boundaries, were originally introduced and developed for real space within traditional-classical human geography, adhering to the regional approach, which dominating geography up to the late 1950s. All of these concepts originally related to space per se rather than to residents and users of specific spaces. However, the interpretation of virtual places offered in Chap. 3, is based on notions that were developed within Marxist, humanist and feminist approaches, which related originally to place residents.

The concepts and terms introduced in Chap. 4 for distance in the Internet are mixed, in terms of their disciplinary origin and period of development. As we will see, distance and distance decay received major attention in the spatial-quantitative paradigm, which dominated Western geography in the 1960s, through the development of models and tools for their conceptualization and measurements under changing geographical conditions. These two concepts too dealt originally mainly with objects in space rather than with people. However, it was for sociologist Anthony Giddens (1990) to innovate the term of distanciation in 1990, as part of his wider theory of structuration, and this concept refers to the relationship between society and space, rather than to objects in space. Proximity, presented also in Chap. 4, jointly with almost all of the terms presented in Chap. 5 for mobility over the Internet, namely flow, speed, directionality, circularity, and co-presence, have all been developed within the interdisciplinary study of mobilities, which has emerged as of the 1990s. All of these concepts and terms deal with dimensions of human individual behavior in space *vis-à-vis* spatial mobility, rather than with space per se or with objects located in space. Finally, it was for geographer Harvey (1989) to define the notion of time-space compression, introduced towards the end of Chap. 5, and referring again to individuals, this time in terms of their experiencing of time and space, when engaged in virtual mobility.

The terminology for Chap. 6, notably for the study of spatial cognition and mental/cognitive mapping for real space, was developed in a variety of disciplines, mainly within behavioral geography, environmental psychology, and architecture. The formative period for the study of spatial cognition was between the 1970s and 1990s. Its extension for cyberspace was proposed at the time by Kwan (2001) and Kellerman (2007).

1.4 Foundations of the Internet

In this section, we will lay down some of the foundations of the Internet: its founders and early adopters, its users, public policies regarding its operations, and some of the 'digital gaps' accompanying its adoption and use by societal sectors, as well as by countries.

1.4.1 The Introduction and Spread of the Internet

The Internet was originally invented in the US in 1969, as ARPANET (Advanced Research Projects Agency Network), consisting at the time of a network of computers which constituted an experimental alternative communications system for telephone services, developed for a potential replacement of the telephone system in case of nuclear disasters. As such, it was originally experimented through a network connecting security headquarters with universities (Kellerman 2002). This experimental network led in the 1970s to the emergence of academic networks (e.g. BITNET (But It's Time Network), and NSFNET (National Science Foundation Network), first connecting among scientists through e-mail, mainly in North American and European universities, and later permitting the uploading of information and data files through the Gopher Protocol.

It took a long period of some 25 years of incubation and development for these early security and academic electronic networks of communications and information, until they matured into a universally open and commercial entity, known as the Internet, back in 1994. However, it took much less time, just seven years following its introduction, in 2001, that the Internet was adopted by one half of Americans, either having access to it, mainly at work or in school, or being online at home. Urry (2003, p. 63) considered the current universal availability of the Internet as the best example for the adoption of a technology for purposes completely different from those envisaged by its developers.

The adoption and use of the Internet has spread globally during the 2000s, so that exposure to cyberspace has turned into a routine daily experience, notably in developed countries. Thus, the ITU (International Telecommunication Union) estimated for 2015, that some 43.4 % of the global population made use of the system (82.2 % in developed countries and just 35.3 % in developing ones) (ITU 2015). Even more impressively, some 95 % of the world population lives in areas currently covered by mobile phone signals (ITU 2015). The ITU further estimated for 2015 that about 47 % of the global population, mainly in developed countries, possessed active mobile broadband subscriptions, a rate which has grown annually by some 40 %! (ITU 2015).

However, there still exists a significant 'digital gap' between developed and developing countries, as far as Internet use is concerned. Thus, some 4 billion people, living in developing countries, are still offline, amounting to some two-thirds of the population in developing countries (ITU 2015). Albeit, this is not the case for the adoption of mobile phones, the use of which does not require literacy and expensive equipment, so that some 97 % of the world population subscribed to this communications means in 2015 (ITU 2015)!

Compared to the diffusion of the fixed-line telephone at the time, the rapid adoption of the Internet, as well as that of mobile telephony, has had to do with the prior existence of partial telecommunications infrastructures for their operations, available through the fixed-line telephone system, so that new connections to the system could be performed relatively easily. Of no less importance, though, has been the emergence of both the Internet and mobile telephony at a time when these innovations constituted technologies and means for the support of the evolving information society, based on information technologies at large. The Internet was based on PCs (personal computers), as well as on the digitization of the previously existing fixed-line telephone system. The idea of the information society, on its part, has implied a special emphasis on the production, processing, transmission, and consumption of information, and the Internet has become a leading system in this regard.

As compared to the Internet, mobile telephony, though, presented a rather slow evolution since the time of its original invention, early after the introduction of the telephone, until its massive adoption as of the 1990s. Mobile telephony had to await for its final development and massive adoption until the release of the required wave spectrum in the late 1960s, when proper social and economic conditions emerged for such a long-awaited move by the American FCC (Federal Communication Commission). As of the 2000s, mobile phones that have been connected to mobile broadband transmission and called ‘smartphones’, have become Internet terminals, similarly to PCs and laptops.

1.4.2 Open Code for the Internet

The Internet has been governed by an *open code*, which Lessig (2001) considered as the ‘heart of the Internet’ (p. 246), and which may be related to its origin in the US, a country which has enjoyed a societal accent on freedom of expression. This open code has provided users with unlicensed access for their production of Internet information, whether through the establishment of websites or through the writing of e-mail messages. It has further permitted an open access to the consumption of Internet information, through the receipt of e-mails, as well as through accessing free of charge websites. The open code principle has further permitted the uncontrolled flows of information from any origins to any destinations, unless sanctioned by governmental censorship. This open code system can also be viewed as facilitating and encouraging the free introduction and innovation of inventions and applications for both the production and consumption of Internet information. All of these activities have been unrestricted neither by a minimal nor by a maximal age of users, so that the use of the Internet constitutes a completely informal activity, as compared, for example, to the requirement for driving licenses at a minimal age for the moving of automobiles in real space.

The open code nature of the Internet has had some additional expressions, for instance in the evolution of some informal e-mail correspondence codes, using alphanumeric signs for smiles, agreement, etc. This trend has matured in chat platforms for mobile phones, such as WhatsApp and Viber, which provide a large variety of ready-made icons. By the very nature of the Internet as a mainly verbal communications system, literacy is much more required for its use than it is for driving, which is based mainly on road signs. Another informal requirement for Internet use is the knowledge of some basic computer operations. A third requirement for Internet use is some knowledge of English, which is almost imperative, as illiteracy of the English language implies no access to information contained in over one-half of the websites (see Hargittai 1999; W^{3}Techs 2015). Thus, the use of the Internet is not only facilitated by its wide accessibility and affordability, but it is also conditioned by the capabilities of its users, as well as by their choices of preferred uses (Kline 2013; Graham et al. 2015).

There are several societal restricting forces for the free use of the Internet. First there are numerous governments that have enforced censorship on the production and consumption of Internet information, thus harming the Internet principle of open code (Warf 2013). Additional restricting forces are culture and religion, functioning as informal dimensions, which may influence the extent of use of the Internet, as well as its open code nature. Such restrictions may be the case notably when religious authorities attempt to restrict access to the system, or when they enforce censorships on its use.

The Internet was considered to constitute 'a metaphor for the social life as fluid' (Urry 2000, p. 40). Thus, the term *Internetness* (Kellerman 2006) was proposed as referring to values, practices, norms and patterns within the three spheres of individuals, society and space, regarding the extent of adoption and use of the Internet. If not used for incoming telephone calls through VoIP (Voice over Internet Protocol), the Internet cannot be considered a time-intruder for its users. In other words, the Internet facilitates its operation by users at any time of their individual choices, but it does not amount to an intrusion or intervention into the time scheduling of communicating parties, as compared to the time-intrusion by incoming telephone calls.

1.4.3 Digital Gaps for the Internet by Country and Gender

The terms 'digital gap' and 'digital divide' have both been coined for wide differences in the adoption of and use of communications media among countries and social sectors. We will use throughout our following discussion the term 'digital gap'.

'The Internet is a social product that is interwoven with relations of class, race, and gender and increasingly subject to the uses of power' (Warf 2006, p. xxvii). Let us demonstrate this wide-ranging statement by focusing on just one specific dimension for a possible digital gap: international gender differences in the very use of the Internet. As expected, the ITU (2015) data on the percentage individuals using the Internet by gender per country reveal that in most countries the percentage of men using the Internet is higher than the equivalent one for women. However, this percentage gap is either negligible or small for most countries. There are, however, two extreme groups of countries with regard to gender differences in the use of the Internet. First, there are those 17 countries in which the percentage men using the Internet is over 5 % higher than that of women (Table 1.1), and second there are those 11 countries in which the percentage of women using the Internet is higher than that of men (Table 1.2).

One would initially expect that the first group of countries, presenting male dominance in Internet use, would consist of developing countries, whereas the second group of countries presenting female dominance in Internet use would be comprised of developed countries. However, this is not the case, and the level of national economic development does not determine gender differences in the

Table 1.1 Countries with significantly higher male Internet penetration*

Country	Year	Percentage male Internet users	Percentage female Internet users
Austria	2013	84.3	77.0
Croatia	2013	74.2	59.9
Germany	2013	86.9	81.5
Greece	2013	63.5	56.3
Iran	2013	33.8	25.8
Italy	2013	63.0	54.0
Japan	2013	84.5	78.0
Korea (South)	2013	88.5	81.0
Morocco	2013	58.3	45.4
Oman	2013	71.2	59.8
Palestinian Authority	2011	44.6	34.4
Peru	2013	42.3	36.0
Portugal	2013	66.3	58.2
Serbia	2009	47.3	36.3
Singapore	2009	72.6	64.5
Switzerland	2013	90.4	82.4
TFYR Macedonia	2012	60.7	54.1

*At least 5 % more than female Internet penetration
Data source ITU (2015)

Table 1.2 Countries with higher female internet penetration

Country	Year	Percentage female internet users	Percentage male internet users
Bahamas	2010	67.0	62.3
Bahrain	2013	104.6	82.2
Brazil	2013	52.8	49.1
Cuba	2013	29.8	25.1
Ireland	2013	78.5	78.0
Jamaica	2012	36.5	31.0
Panama	2012	41.9	38.6
Slovakia	2013	78.2	77.6
Thailand	2013	29.1	28.8
United States	2011	70.1	69.4
Venezuela	2012	50.6	47.5

Data source ITU (2015)

percentage users of the Internet. By its very nature, the use of the Internet is a matter of personal choice and affordability, but, still, the aggregate decisions on the use of the Internet may reflect national tendencies, as far as exposures of women to information, to social communications, and to finances and shopping are concerned. In some other countries, the level of female participation in Internet activities may depend on their level of literacy as compared to that of men. In light of these tendencies, let us now examine the particular countries included in the two groups of male and female dominance in Internet use.

Table 1.1 presents three global spheres with a significantly higher share of men using the Internet: Mediterranean countries, including European, North African and Middle Eastern ones; German speaking countries; and East Asian countries that have led the emergence of information society. Data on the distribution of Internet users by gender and age for Germany (Statista 2015a) and for Japan (Statista 2015b) in 2015, reveal that the general trend of male dominance probably reflects male dominance among Internet users aged over 54, a population sector which constitutes a growing share of the population in these two countries. This group may represent in large part, more conservative social values. Probably the same would apply also to the rest of the developed countries included in these three groups of countries, though data on Internet usage by age group have not been available to validate this assumption. As far as other countries, mainly the Muslim ones, male dominance in Internet use may reflect cultural trends and preferences with regard to women's exposures to some or all of the opportunities offered by the Internet: information, communications and Internet activities.

Table 1.2, which presents the opposite trend, namely countries with female dominance in the use of the Internet, includes one major group, that of Latin American and Caribbean countries, coupled with several individual countries from other parts of the world. Thus, in numerous Latin American countries more women enjoy a wider communications sphere than men do. This tendency regarding the use of the Internet constitutes just one aspect of a more general trend reported by the

World Economic Forum reports, namely that 'Latin America and the Caribbean is the region that has made the most progress at closing the gender gap over the last ten years' (Ugarte 2015; compare with Warf 2009).

1.5 Internet Social Spatiality

At the basis of our attempt to view the Internet and its three spaces as categories of image space which can be interpreted and analyzed using real space parameters, lies the assumption that Internet cyberspace can be considered as constituting a special form of social space, as reflected in several of its uses and applications. This applies foremost to the Web, or the Internet information space. Thus, for example, cyberspace on the Web constitutes a resource and a production force, similarly to real space, for instance in its provision for online shopping. Internet cyberspace can further be considered as text and as symbol for individual users as well as for organizations and companies that own websites. The Web may further be looked upon as constituting a landscape, as portrayed on computer screens. Both the information and communications spaces of the Internet may involve some social values in their ways of usage by individuals (see Dodge and Kitchin 2001 for detailed discussions).

As we will see in the following chapters, the Internet enjoys its own spatialities, expressed through the operations performed by designers and owners of cyber spatial entities, namely communications platforms and websites, as well as through activities carried out by their individual and institutional users. As such, the Internet constitutes social space, similarly to human made real space. These two social spaces, the real and the virtual, have been discussed in detail elsewhere (Kellerman 2014). Thus, in the following paragraphs, as well as in Table 1.3, we would like to present the essence of these two social spaces. This is of some importance since we will focus in Chaps. 3–6 on concepts and terms extended from real space to the Internet.

Social space theory has been primarily based on Lefebvre's (1991) view of space as constituting simultaneously material entity, product and symbol. Based on this multiple connotations of space, Lefebvre (1991) presented a most insightful sociospatial classification for the wide-ranging human experiencing of space (see also Merrifield 1993; Kirsch 1995). He, thus, differentiated among material spatial practices, the representations of space, and the spaces of representations, jointly constituting human social spatiality. These relations were interpreted by Harvey (1989, pp. 220–221) as relating to human (direct) spatial experiences (for material spatial practices), the perception of space by individuals (for the representation of space), and the imagination of space (for the spaces of representation). Harvey (1989) provided further detail to the spatial expressions of these relations under varying spatial practices: accessibility and distanciation; appropriation and use; domination and control; and production of space. Soja (1996) interpreted Lefebvre's three classes a bit differently, by claiming that they constitute a trialectic,

Table 1.3 Real and cyber social spaces

Dimension	Real social space	Cyber social space
Spatial practices *Performed* through flows, transfers, and interactions	**Routine activities** *Performed* by individuals in distinct geographical scales, mainly, but not only, locally	**Routine activities** *Performed* by individuals through the Internet in instantly integrated spatial scales, topped by globalization, and using geographical language
Representations of space *Constructed* through the implementation of codes and knowledge	**Professional designing** *Constructed* by spatial sciences (e.g. planning), and dominated by distances in, and terrain of, pre-existing space	**Professional designing** *Constructed* by computing specialists, dominated by networking and linking, and space is created only through the construction of websites
Spaces of representation *Presented* through ideas, images and symbols	**Artistic and literal work** *Presented* by artists, writers and philosophers	**Graphic design** *Presented* by graphics specialists, aiming at imagined materialization of virtual space

Source Following Kellerman (2014) (Table 2.1)

which consists of human perception (or *Firstspace*), human conception (or *Secondspace*), and people's living of space (or *Thirdspace*), respectively (see also Kellerman 2014).

Table 1.3 presents a comparison of real and virtual spaces from the perspective of the three dimensions developed originally for the spatialities experienced by people with regard to real space. The extension of these spatialities for virtual space, which is presented in the table, is partially based on notions proposed by Weinberger (2002) and Meishar-Tal (2006). The first dimension, namely spatial practices, relates to the ongoing, daily and routine activities of individuals. In real space, these activities are normally carried out within the local sphere, unless out of town travel is performed, whereas Internet routine activities present a continuous blend of activities performed locally, domestically and globally. These routine virtual activities are performed through communications channels, as well as through the consultation of websites.

The second dimension of spatiality, the representation of space, involves, for real space, the professional design of real space constructs (such as homes, roads, etc.), and it is based on the application of codes and knowledge which are commonly in use among planners. Such design activities are constrained by terrain and distances, or the pre-existing space. The equivalent design activities for the representation of Internet cyberspace are the design activities performed by computer specialists for the construction of websites. Such design projects for the Internet are not constrained by preexisting space, but they are expected to connect, link, and network with preexisting websites.

The difference between real space and cyberspace is striking even more when it comes to the spaces of representation. In real space, this relates to artistic and literal works portraying pieces of space. By their very nature, such artistic and literal works are completely free in their style and ways of artistic and literal expressions, depending only on the individual minds of artists, authors and thinkers. The notion of spaces of representation for the Internet is of a different nature. A website designed by computer specialists is composed of codes written in computer languages, possibly accompanied by some most basic graphical presentations. It is, then, for graphics and arts specialists to turn these coded websites into meaningful, attractive, and easy to operate computer screens for their users, employing professional knowledge and rules, side by side with free style artistic creativity.

We have identified so far three types of actors for social spaces, differentially for real and virtual spaces: designers of spatial facilities, users of these spatial facilities, and interpreters for these facilities. We have now to add a fourth one, namely the owners of spatial facilities, who may determine the very nature and the function of specific spatial facilities. In real space, owners of spatial facilities can be governments, responsible for the construction of, for instance, roads and schools; businesses, owning facilities, such as stores; and individuals, owning their residential homes. Similarly, in cyberspace, websites may represent owners who offer services, both governmental and business ones, side by side with individuals owning personal websites and blogs.

In summary, and towards our detailed discussions in Chaps. 2–6, Table 1.4 lists the geographical concepts, or the geographical parameters, for the interpretation of the Internet, by their order of presentation in the upcoming chapters. The table further presents the agents who operate or use each of these parameters, out of the four ones discussed above (users, computing specialists, graphic designers, and owners). In addition, the table presents the ways of operation for each of the agents per each parameter, and these will be discussed in detail in the following chapters. As for virtual space, the role of users is dominant in the operation of the Internet, so that they eventually determine in numerous ways their own individual operational geographies in cyberspace.

1.6 Terrestrial Geography of the Internet

The numerous dimensions of the Internet terrestrial geography have been presented in detail elsewhere (e.g. Kellerman 2002; Malecki and Moriset 2008; Tranos 2013; Kellerman 2014), so that it will suffice here to note only briefly on them. In our discussions so far, we have met already several aspects of the Internet terrestrial geography, such as the distribution of Internet users by country and gender. Additional terrestrial dimensions of the Internet geography consist of the location and distribution patterns for Internet facilities located in real space, other than devices for personal Internet usage, such as PCs, tablets and smart phones. These facilities include website hosting and transmission systems, and their spatial patterns are outlined in the following paragraphs.

Table 1.4 Actors and operations for internet geographical dimensions

Dimension	Operator	Way of operation
Chapter 3		
Ground	Graphic designer	Design of screen background, and creating screen information density
Place	User Owner	Users' feelings, social relations and performances in non-places Investment for revenues
Regions	Owner	Contents visual organization by number of pages
Boundaries	Owner Government	Visual organization of contents, and restricted website access Censorship
Chapter 4		
Distance	Owner and computing designer	Number of clicks within and between websites
Distance decay	1. System 2. Owner 3. User	1. Latency in website contacting 2. On screen ordering of search results 3. Physical distance to contacts
Distanciation	User	The spatial extent of consulted websites and of social contacts
Proximity	User	Choice of communications media by levels of social relationships
Chapter 5		
Flow	Computing designer	Efficiency and friendliness of screen sequences
Speed	Owner	Information transmission speeds
Directionality	User	Disinterest in geographical addresses of accessed websites and addressees, but interest in message recipients and website contents
Circularity	User	Session beginning and ending at homepage, often also repetitive uses of specific websites at routine times
Co-presence	User	Simultaneous presence in physical and virtual locations for the access of people, events, places, information, and things
Time-space compression	User	Communicating with people in places at other time zones
Chapter 6		
Cognition	User	Partial cognition of information and communications spaces, but no cognitive mapping

See also Kellerman (2016), Table 1

Websites are normally hosted by Internet hosting servers, and these servers are concentrated in Internet hotels or Internet farms, which are properly equipped (e.g. with fine-tuned air-conditioning) and monitored (for proper functioning and against mal-practicing). The US is the dominant country in website hosting, with some 68.3 % of the websites worldwide hosted there in 2015 (Web Hosting 2016).

Following their design, registration and hosting, websites are ready for access by users through the Internet transmission system. This system consists of four major layers: the physical layer; data link; network layer; and transport (Gorman and Malecki 2001). Generally and in simplified words, the establishment of connection by users, followed by data transmission from and to their computers or smartphones in sessions of Internet use, proceeds along the following process. A user approaches the system through the physical layer, which constitutes the web of lines connecting computers worldwide, separately or jointly with the system of telephone lines. When an Internet user calls for a website, which is located in a hosting server, using her/his end station (a computer or a smart phone), this call is normally executed through the user's Internet Service Provider (ISP). The data link of the ISP checks the unique numerical IP (Internet Protocol) address of the called server and its location on the network. Then, the network link (or the network layer), and its routers, establish the best path for moving data between the calling and called computers. In the next step, an interactive session or reliable transport of data begins.

Domestic, international and intercontinental transmissions of Internet information are channeled through 'Internet backbones', which serve as 'highways' for Internet traffic, similarly to the road or airline traffic systems. Long distance, international and intercontinental Internet data are transmitted either through satellites, or through the maritime fiberoptic cable system, which is monitored by Internet exchanges. Both of these systems have their own geographies. The satellite system covers the whole planet, including the oceans, thus providing Internet access also for sailors and boat travelers. The maritime fiber optic cable system connects all the continents with significantly high cable capacity across the Atlantic Ocean. Much of the global Internet traffic is still routed through the US, which enjoys the heaviest routing and exchange system, so that the US dominates several components of the Internet economy: the registration of websites (as we will see in Chap. 3), their hosting, and the transmission of information to and from them (Kellerman 2014).

1.7 Conclusion

The following chapters will introduce concepts for the geographic interpretation of the Internet, jointly proposing a systematic geographic interpretation for the system and its components. The concepts which will be presented in the following chapters were originally proposed and used for the analysis of real space, and they are conceptually experimented here for their possible extension for the cyber spatial Internet. Thus, the book proposes, and if only a posteriori, some possible transcendence of terminology from real space to cyberspace. This transcendence may further point to some possible combination between terrestrial and virtual geographies. We will return to this point in Chap. 7, the concluding chapter for the book.

The following chapter will present the set of image spaces, to which the Internet belongs. The terms and concepts that will be discussed in Chaps. 3–6 are substantive, rather than methodological ones, and they were developed originally within several geographical epistemologies. The concepts which are introduced in Chap. 3 for the structure of Internet cyberspace, were originally introduced and developed for real space by the regional approach. The concepts and terms introduced in Chap. 4 for distance in the Internet are mixed, in terms of their disciplinary origin and period of development, evolving either through the spatial-quantitative paradigm, or, as is the case for distanciation, as part of the sociological theory of structuration. Proximity, presented also in Chap. 4, jointly with almost all of the terms presented in Chap. 5 for mobility over the Internet, have been developed within the interdisciplinary study of mobilities, emerging as of the 1990s. All of these latter concepts deal with dimensions of human individual behavior in space *vis-à-vis* spatial mobility. Finally, time-space compression discussed also in Chap. 5 refers again to individuals. The terminology for Chap. 6, notably for the study of spatial cognition and mental/cognitive mapping for real space, was developed mainly within the fields of behavioral geography, environmental psychology, and architecture.

The Internet has been one of the fastest diffusing and adopted innovations, introduced originally back in 1969, and maturing into an open code and universally available system, as of 1994. There are still 'digital gaps' in the adoption of the system, both globally between developed and developing countries, as well as domestically within societal sectors, such as age and gender. The international differences in the rates of Internet adoption between men and women depend on age group, culture and policy, and not necessarily on differences in levels of national economic development. The US dominates the registration and hosting of websites, as well as the transmission of information to and from them.

The social space of the Internet consists of four types of actors: users, computer specialists, website graphic designers, and site owners, all of whom serve as Internet actors. However, the social space of the Internet lacks the artistic, literal and philosophical descriptions and representations of space, which typify the representations of real space. The numerous dimensions which will be discussed in Chaps. 3–6 may be divided by the actors that operate them, and it is, to a large degree, for users to eventually shape their own personal cyberspatial geographies of action.

References

Adams, P. (1998). Network topologies and virtual place. *Annals of the Association of American Geographers, 88*, 88–106.

Adams, P. C., & Ghose, R. (2003). India.com: The construction of a space between. *Progress in Human Geography, 27*, 414–437.

Avidan, I., & Kellerman, A. (2004). Distance in the Internet by time and route: An empirical examination. *Horizons (Contemporary Israeli Geography), 60–61*, 77–88.

Batty, M. (1997). Virtual geography. *Futures, 29*, 337–352.
Benedikt, M. (1991). Cyberspace: Some proposals. In M. Benedikt (Ed.), *Cyberspace: First steps* (pp. 119–224). Cambridge, MA: MIT Press.
Cai, G., Hirtle, S., & Williams, J. (1999). Mapping the geography of cyberspace using telecommunications infrastructure information. *The First international workshop on telegeo-processing*. http://spatial.ist.psu.edu/cai/cai-1999-Telegeo.pdf.
Couclelis, H. (no date, probably 1997). *The naïve geography of cyberspace*. http://www.ncgia.buffalo.edu/i21/papers/cook2.
Crang, M., Crang, P., & May, J. (1999). Introduction. In M. Crang, P. Crang, & J. May (Eds.), *Virtual geographies: Bodies, space and relations* (pp. 1–13). London: Routledge.
Dodge, M. (1999). *The Geographies of cyberspace*. University College London Centre for Advanced Spatial Analysis (CASA), Working Paper Series 8. http://discovery.ucl.ac.uk/266/1/cyberspace.pdf.
Dodge, M. (2001). Guest editorial. *Environment and Planning B: Planning and Design, 28*, 1–2.
Dodge, M., & Kitchin, R. (2001). *Mapping cyberspace*. London: Routledge.
Earle, C., Mathewson, K., & Kenzer, M. S. (Eds.). (1996). Introduction back to basics: The virtues of key concepts in human geography. *Concepts in human geography* (pp. xi–xxv). Lanham, MD: Rowman and Littlefield.
Giddens, A. (1990). *The Consequences of modernity*. Cambridge: Polity Press.
Gorman, S. P., & Malecki, E. J. (2001). Fixed and fluid: Stability and change in the geography of the internet. Paper presented at the annual meeting of the association of American geographers, New York.
Graham, M., de Sabbata, S., & Zook, M. A. (2015). Towards a study of information geographies: (Im)mutable augmentations and a mapping of the geographies of information. *Geo: Geography and environment*, *2*, 88–105.
Hargittai, E. (1999). Weaving the Western web: Explaining differences in Internet connectivity among OECD countries. *Telecommunications Policy, 23*, 701–718.
Harvey, D. (1989). *The Condition of postmodernity*. Oxford: Blackwell.
Holloway, S. I., & Valentine, G. (2001). Placing cyberspace: Processes of Americanization in British children's use of the interne. *Area, 33*, 153–160.
ITU (International Telecommunication Union). (2015). Aggregate data. http://www.itu.int/en/ITU-D/Statistics/Pages/stat/default.aspx.
Kellerman, A. (2002). *The internet on earth: A geography of information*. London and New York: Wiley.
Kellerman, A. (2006). *Personal mobilities*. London and New York: Routledge.
Kellerman, A. (2007). Cyberspace classification and cognition: Information and communications cyberspaces. *Journal of Urban Technology, 14*, 5–32.
Kellerman, A. (2014). *The Internet as second action space*. London and New York: Routledge.
Kellerman, A. (2016). Image spaces and the geography of internet screen-space. *Geojournal, 81* (forthcoming), doi: 10.1007/s10708-015-9639-1.
Kinsley, S. (2014). The matter of 'virtual' geographies. *Progress in Human Geography, 38*, 364–384.
Kirsch, S. (1995). The incredible shrinking world? Technology and the production of space. *Environment and Planning D: Society and Space, 13*, 529–555.
Kitchin, R., & Dodge, M. (2011). *Code/space: Software and everyday life*. Cambridge, MA: MIT Press.
Kline, D. (2013). *Technologies of choice? ICTs, development, and the capabilities approach*. Cambridge, MA: MIT Press.
Kwan, M.-P. (2001). Cyberspatial cognition and individual access to information: The behavioral foundation of cybergeography. *Environment and Planning B, 28*, 21–37.
Lefebvre, H. (1991). *The production of space* (D. Nicholson-Smith, Trans.). Oxford: Basil Blackwell.
Lessig, L. (2001). *The future of ideas: The fate of the commons in a connected world*. New York: Random House.

Li, F., Whalley, J., & Williams, H. (2001). Between physical and electronic spaces: The implications for organizations in the networked economy. *Environment and Planning A, 33*, 699–716.

Loo, B. P. Y. (2012). *The E-society*. New York: Nova.

Malecki, E. J., & Moriset, B. (2008). *The digital economy: Business organization, production processes and regional developments*. London and New York: Routledge.

Meishar-Tal, H. (2006). The Internet and social dynamics. Unpublished doctoral dissertation. Department of Geography, University of Haifa (Hebrew).

Merrifield, A. (1993). Place and space: A Lefebvrian reconciliation. *Transactions of the British Institute of Geographers, 18*, 516–531.

Paterson, M. (2006). Feel the presence: Technologies of touch and distance. *Environment and Planning D: Society and Space, 24*, 691–708.

Péruch, P., Gaunet, F., Thinus-Blanc, C., & Loomis, J. (2000). Understanding and learning virtual spaces. In R. Kitchin & S. Freundschuh (Eds.), *Cognitive mapping: Past, present, and future* (pp. 108–115). London: Routledge.

Pickles, J. (2004). *A History of spaces: Cartographic reason, mapping and the geo-coded world*. London and New York: Routledge.

Soja, E. W. (1996). *Thirdspace: Journeys to Los Angeles and other real-and-imagined places*. Cambridge, MA: Blackwell.

Statista, The Statistics Portal. (2015a). Share of internet users in Germany in May 2015, by age and gender. http://www.statista.com/statistics/442483/internet-users-by-age-and-gender-germany/.

Statista, The Statistics Portal. (2015b). Distribution of internet users in Japan as of May 2015, by age group and gender. http://www.statista.com/statistics/478611/age-gender-distribution-of-internet-users-in-japan/.

Tranos, E. (2013). *The geography of the internet: Cities, regions and internet infrastructure in Europe*. Northampton, MA: Edward Edgar.

Ugarte, P. P. (2015). Top 10 most gender equal countries in Latin America and the Caribbean. World Economic Forum Agenda. https://agenda.weforum.org/2015/11/top-10-most-gender-equal-countries-in-latin-america-and-the-caribbean-2/.

Urry, J. (2000). *Sociology beyond societies: Mobilities for the twenty-first century*. London: Routledge.

Urry, J. (2003). *Global complexity*. Cambridge: Polity.

W^3Techs. (2015). Usage of contents languages for websites. http://w3techs.com/technologies/overview/content_language/all.

Wang, Y., Lai, P., & Sui, D. (2003). Mapping the Internet using GIS: The death of distance hypothesis revisited. *Journal of Geographical Systems, 5*, 381–405.

Warf, B. (Ed.). (2006). Introduction. *Encyclopedia of human geography* (pp. xxv–xxviii). Thousand Oaks, CA: SAGE.

Warf, B. (2009). Diverse spatialities of the Latin American and Caribbean Internet. *Journal of Latin American geography, 8*, 125–145.

Warf, B. (2013). *Global geographies of the internet*. Dordrecht: Springer.

Web Hosting. (2016). Hosting stats by country. http://webhosting.info/web-hosting.

Weinberger, D. (2002). *Small pieces loosely joined {a unified theory of the web}*. Cambridge, MA: Perseus.

Chapter 2
The Internet as Space

Abstract This chapter will, first, present the general notion of image space, and a scalar model differentiating among its four visual classes: virtual space (visual presentations of real space and material artifacts), cyberspace (digital communications and information media), the Internet (digital communications and informational spaces), and Internet screen-space (users' visual interface with the Internet). This scalar model leads from the wider to the specific. This differentiation will be followed by discussions of cyberspace and Internet screen-space geography.

Keywords Image space · Virtual space · Cyberspace · The internet · Internet information space · Internet communications space · Internet screen-space

Our journey into the specific geographical dimensions of the cyberspatial Internet will begin in this chapter, with an exploration of the most basic geographical concept, namely space, as manifested in image spaces. Thus, we will discuss, first, the rather wide and general notion of image space. We will then move to the presentation of a scalar model that will differentiate among its four visual classes, from the wider to the specific. First, virtual space—the visual presentations of real space and material artifacts. Second, cyberspace—the digital communications and information media. Third, the Internet—or digital communications and informational spaces, and finally and fourth, Internet screen-space—the visual interface between Internet information and communications spaces and their users (Fig. 2.1).

In this scalar model, virtual space constitutes the widest term, hence including cyberspace, which on its part includes the Internet and its screens, or its user interfaces, which we call the Internet screen-spaces. The discussions of these four classes of image space will focus on differences among them, as well as on relationships among them, rather than attempting to put these four classes into the context of spatial theory concepts that were developed originally for real space. Following the exploration of the scalar model for image spaces, we will continue our discussion with a discussion of the geographies of Internet information, communications and screen spaces.

A. Kellerman, *Geographic Interpretations of the Internet*,
SpringerBriefs in Geography, DOI 10.1007/978-3-319-33804-0_2

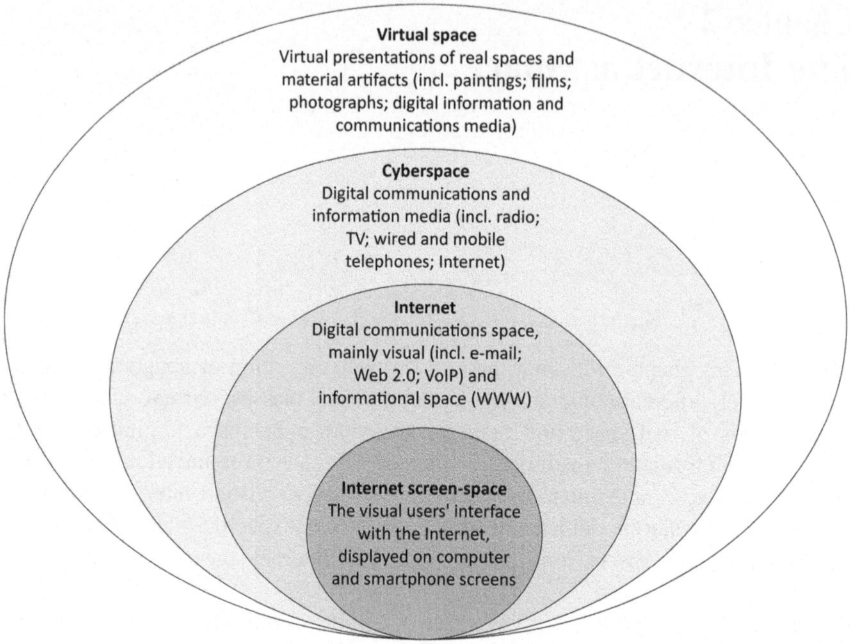

Fig. 2.1 Image space classes. *Source* Based on Kellerman (2016), Fig. 1 (with permission)

2.1 Image Space

The common denominator among virtual, cyber, and Internet spaces is that they all constitute image spaces. Images are normally conceived of as visual representations of material entities, but as Jay (1994, pp. 8–9) noted: 'There is [therefore] something revealing in the ambiguities surrounding the word 'image', which can signify graphic, optical, perceptual, mental or verbal phenomena'. Aumont (1997) distinguished among three channels for image space expressions: spectators' perceptions, image transmission apparatuses, and the images themselves. For the latter class he focused on painting, film and photography, noting generally, 'that space is a much more complex category than its iconic representation' (p. 160), and thus requiring several adjustments for its image presentation, notably the need to use perspective.

Within geography, images were initially attributed to mental images, i.e. imagined spaces, and their visual expression through mental maps (Phillips 1993; Chap. 6). Later on, interest moved to space in pre-cinematic and cinematic film technologies (e.g., Doel and Clarke 2005), and even to slides (Rose 2003) and diagrams (Petersson 2005). The common thread among these latter explorations is their engagement mainly with the expression and treatment of real space within certain media, rather than on these media as constituting spaces by themselves.

Our interest here is to look at classes of images as spaces by themselves, with a distinct focus on Internet spaces. Ash (2009) paved an initial road in this direction in his study of video game screens as spaces. He assumed that space in visual images 'can be considered as a surface, a flat image presented on the screen' (Ash 2009, p. 211). Ash (2009) further developed several notions regarding visual image spaces, tying together the distinct classes that Aumont (1997) proposed and that we mentioned before. First among these notions is that images represent the real world, even if in skewed, distorted, or imagined forms, but simultaneously they also produce and create spaces. Second, 'the 'being' of images consists of both a *materiality* and a *phenomenality*, which both act in concert, as the conditions for being able to 'see' or experience the image at all' (Ash 2009, pp. 2107–2108). Third, image spatiality is an existential one, because it is constructed by the activities and engagement of image users. Image spaces constitute, therefore, two things at once: imagined spaces as perceived by image users, and material or visual images representing real space.

Image spaces include also metaphorical spaces, traditionally referring to the spaces that are presented and verbally described in non-visual literal texts, mainly in prose and poetry writings. Contemporarily, though, metaphorical spaces may include also digital visual entities and representations, notably the Internet information and communications spaces. Hence, we noted already the wide application of spatial notions for the use of the Internet (e.g., site, home, surfing, etc.) (see e.g., Schlottmann and Miggelbrink 2009). In addition to these metaphorical spatial expressions for the very use of the Internet, the visual expression of the Internet through Internet screens may also be considered as image spaces. Thus, we may differentiate among four classes of virtual image spaces, nesting within each other: virtual space; cyberspace; the Internet information and communications spaces; and Internet screen space. We will now examine these four classes of visual image spaces, focusing on their specific qualities and on geographical notions pertaining to the understanding of each of them.

2.2 Virtual Space

The two terms of cyberspace and virtual space may seem at first glance as synonyms, notably if both terms are perceived as being exclusively digital (see e.g., Graham 2005; Tranos and Nijkamp 2013). Kinsley (2014, p. 365), in his review of virtuality, noted the nuanced range of interpretations for virtual space as a digital entity. Thus, 'the 'virtual' of 'virtual geographies' tends to mean simulation of a kind of digital liminality, akin to a space 'between' screen and body, data and machine' (see also Crang et al. 1999, p. 6).

Following Ettlinger (2008), and see also the discussion by Grosz (2001, pp. 78–81), we suggest that virtual space constitutes a much wider entity than cyberspace, so that digital cyberspace constitutes its subset. As Ettlinger (2008) claimed 'virtual space is the visible world of pictorial images: paintings, films, photographs, TV programs, video games, or any other pictorial medium—i.e. physical devices that allow us to experience through them something that is not physically there' (p. xi). Thus, 'virtual space is not the world of dreams' and 'virtual space is not a hallucination' (p. 31), whereas 'referring to the Internet in terms of a space, [therefore,] is valid only metaphorically—as a conceptual type of space' (p. 27), and 'cyberspace with all its complexity and elaboration is only a specifically-defined subset of virtual space' (p. 33).

Still, though, the very nature of the virtual, and even more so its geography, are complex, since it is difficult to interpret them along the classical differentiation between abstract and relative spaces (see e.g., Curry 1998), with virtual space possibly presenting a merge between these two classes of space (Hillis 1999, p. 77). The experiencing of virtual space might get close to but will never be identical to that of real space (Crang et al. 1999). The interpretation of the virtual as something 'which is not physical but emulates the physical' was attributed by Farman (2012, p. 37) to 17th century Christianity.

Virtual space is coupled, by its very nature, with the process of virtualization, studied at the time by Lévy (1998), who noted that 'when a person, community, act, or piece of information are virtualized, they are 'not-there', they deterritorialize themselves' (p. 29), and 'if cyberspace results from the virtualization of computers, the electronic highway reifies this virtual world' (p. 160). Virtualization, thus, amounts to a *process* of turning things into the virtual, and this process is independent of cyberspace as a specific class of virtual *entity*. In other words, virtualization implies a *process* of transformation of things, whereas cyberspace denotes a *condition* of visual exhibition of virtual things, mainly through television and the Internet. Hence, turning something into a virtual condition does not necessarily imply its being presented over cyberspace, but the opposite case is true: things which are presented on cyberspace are always virtual.

2.3 Cyberspace

The essence of our following discussion is an attempt to cope with the question: 'Is cyberspace a kind of space?' (Adams and Warf 1997, p. 141), notably since 'cyberspace has been considered a 'parallel' universe to our own' (Grosz 2001, p. 76). In its being a space for itself, cyberspace has been viewed as neither absolute nor relative (Wang et al. 2003). Gibson (1984) originally proposed the term 'cyberspace' as a science-fiction notion, and this notion was applied later to computer-mediated communications, as well as to virtual reality technologies (Kitchin 1998a, p. 2). The specific conceptions of cyberspace as a geographical concept and entity have received wide interpretations. Cyberspace was, thus, seen as synonymous with information space in general (as reviewed by Thrift 1996). It was further viewed as a space 'invisible to our senses' (Batty 1993, p. 615), and it was accepted as a geographic metaphor for disembodiment (Adams 1997; Tranos and Nijkamp 2013). It was also related to as 'a multi-media skein of digital networks' (Graham 1998, p. 165). In addition, Thrift argued for information spaces to 'signal new spatial logics which respect none of the apparently Newtonian constructs of space… They are connected to the rise of images and signs as the means by which our society makes sense of itself' (Thrift 1996, p. 1467). Side by side with these non-material views of cyberspace, it is still spatially and materially based through its real space infrastructure (Zook et al. 2004), and it further interacts with real environments (Light 1999; Graham 1998).

Cyberspace has also been variously defined from spatial perspectives since the early 1990s (see also Kellerman 2014):

1. *Artificial reality*: 'Cyberspace is a globally networked, computer-sustained, computer-accessed, and computer-generated, multidimensional, artificial, or 'virtual', reality' (Benedikt 1991, p. 122; see also Kitchin 1998a, p. 2).
2. *Interactivity space*: 'Interactivity between remote computers defines cyberspace…cyberspace is not necessarily imagined space—it is real enough in that it is the space set up by those who use remote computers to communicate' (Batty 1997, p. 343–344).
3. *Conceptual space*: 'The *conceptual space* within ICTs (information and communication technologies), rather than the technology itself' (Dodge and Kitchin 2001, p. 1).
4. *Metaphorical space*: 'the idea of 'cyberspace' is deployed as an inherently geographic metaphor' (Graham 2013, p. 178).

The first three definitions locate cyberspace within the wide sphere of information technologies, hence including also communications media, i.e. radio, television, and fixed and mobile communications technologies, all of which were originally invented prior to the invention of computers in the late 1940s. The Internet is, therefore, a different medium in this regard, since it has been computer-based as of its original innovation in the 1960s. All of these four definitions relate to cyberspace from the perspective of users' experiences, with cyberspace being viewed as an artificial reality, as a communications platform, or as conceptual or metaphorical spaces.

As such, the four definitions may be considered as complementary to each other, so that cyberspace may be viewed in general as constituting simultaneously a virtual, interactive, conceptual and metaphorical spatial entity. Such a pluralistic approach to the nature of cyberspace is in line with Strate's (1999, p. 383) suggestion that cyberspace is 'better understood as a plurality rather than a singularity'. Strate (1999) further proposed to rank the meanings or building blocks of cyberspace through ranked orders. Zero order refers to the ontological nature of cyberspace as a virtual reality. First order cyberspace relates to the physical space of its hardware, side by side with its being a conceptual space that mediates between its ontological and physical dimensions. Finally, second order cyberspace constitutes a synthesis between the two lower orders.

So far, we have viewed cyberspace as a space for itself, but cyberspace can also be viewed from additional perspectives, as well. Thus, cyberspace may be perceived as exhibiting representations of real space through maps, pictures and graphs, used for the study of real space, and for navigation in real space (Zook and Graham 2007; Zook et al. 2004). Cyberspace was further defined from non-geographical user-oriented perspectives. Hence, for Mitchell (1995, p. 8) 'cyberspace is profoundly *antispatial*', whereas for Mizrach (1996) it constitutes a 'consensual hallucination'. Thus, 'under the right conditions, cyberspace becomes a dream world, not unlike the world which emerges when we sink to sleep' (Suler 1999). However, Internet users can consciously navigate within the publicly available cyberspatial world, the Web, as opposed to dreamers' unconscious navigations within their dream-cyberspace.

Side by side with these non-spatial approaches to the nature of cyberspace, we noted already the application of geographical-spatial daily notions and metaphors for the construction, naming and use of cyberspace, notably for the use of the Internet. This use of geographical terms for the very operation of the Internet received a universal adoption, given the everyday convenience and familiarity of people with real space. Hence, the emergence of Internet terms such as site, browsing, and moving (Wilken 2007; Graham 2013).

The wide adoption of spatial terms for the routine use of cyberspace via the Internet attests to a process of spatialization (Kellerman 2007), implying the adoption of space as a metaphor for cyberspace and its operation. Couclelis (1998) noted on this use of metaphors that it involves 'the mapping of one domain of experience into another, more coherent, powerful, or familiar one…the metaphor performs a cognitive fusion between the two, so that the things in the source domain are viewed as if they really belonged in the target domain' (pp. 214–215). Wide-ranging metaphors were generally termed by Lakoff and Johnson (1980, p. 14) as *orientational metaphors*, and this term seems an obvious case for the adoption of the wide-ranging spatial metaphors for cyberspace and its use. The emergence of the spatial metaphors for cyberspace was further claimed to be founded on the human experience since 'early in life and is essential for survival' (Tversky 2000, p. 76; see also Couclelis 1998). In addition, the spatial metaphor has turned out to be convenient for numerous dimensions of information use: organization, access, integration, and operation (Tversky 2001).

2.4 The Internet

The Internet is foremost a specific cyberspatial communications and informational technology, typified by visual presentations of information to its subscribers. As for its status *vis-à-vis* the real space world, it was suggested that 'the Internet can be thought of as a space attached to the earth' (Wang et al. 2003, p. 383). We traced briefly the history and development of the Internet in Chap. 1 (see also Kellerman 2002), so that it will suffice here to note several classifications for its internal structure. Most basically, and as mentioned already in Chap. 1, the Internet can be divided into its two major functions or components: information space consisting mainly of the Web and its websites, and communications space, which includes mainly e-mail platforms and Web 2.0 social networking applications, led by Facebook and Twitter (Kellerman 2007). We will discuss these two classes of space in some detail in the following two sub-sections, alongside with the Internet screen spaces, which serve as user interfaces with the information and communications spaces. It is important, though, to note once again that both the information and communications spaces of the Internet are virtual, and their constitution as spaces is rather metaphorical. These two metaphorical spaces become visually reified to their users through the Internet screen spaces.

Another basic classification for the Internet is its division into domain names marked by organizational and national signifiers/codes. These codes comprise an integral component for both the specific website addresses and the personal communications addresses (see e.g., Wilson 2001; Chap. 3).

The Internet has been widely viewed as a unique social landscape, being comprised of spatial elements. For example, 'the Internet, as a platform for *virtual interactions* among individuals and organizations, has necessarily a geographical component' (Tranos and Nijkamp 2013, p. 855), and 'the only communication medium that rivals the topological flexibility of computer networks is place itself' (Adams 1998, p. 93). A growingly important element of Internet communications, notably since the wide adoption of social networking platforms (such as Facebook), is the ability for users to communicate anonymously and in most egalitarian ways. As was noted already by Lévy before the construction of Web 2.0, 'here we no longer encounter people exclusively by their name, geographical location, or social rank, but in the context of centers of interest, within a shared landscape of meaning and knowledge' (Lévy 1998, p. 141). Moreover, 'cyberspace provides social spaces that are purportedly free of the constraints of the body; you are accepted on the basis of your written words, not what you look like or sound like' (Kitchin 1998b, pp. 386–387; see also Mizrach 1996).

As mentioned already previously, the Internet consists of three types of spaces: information, communications, and screens. We will look now at each of these spaces separately.

2.4.1 Internet Information Space

We noted already that information space refers to digital information sets or systems, consisting of information organized within metaphorical spatial contexts such as websites, and, hence, involving the use of some additional geographical metaphors such as home, and navigation/surfing. However, information cyberspace includes also digital information sets, such as data archives and library catalogs

(Fabrikant and Buttenfield 2001; Couclelis 1998). All the information sets that are included in the Internet information space are textual and/or graphic in nature, and they have some constancy in terms of their virtual availability to users, so that they may be recalled by their users whenever they find it necessary. Most of these information files are meant to be shared by users: either the general public through the Internet, or segmented and permitted users only, through Intranets. Contemporary search engines have allowed for easy access to websites and files, and as we will discuss in Chap. 4, Google has emerged as a leading service in this regard, providing also searches into more specialized information systems, such as satellite images, and scientific articles and books. Google was, thus, assessed as a megaproject within another megaproject (the Internet) (Paradiso 2011).

2.4.2 Internet Communications Space

The second class of cyberspace is communications space, referring to the cyberspace of individuals who communicate with each other via numerous modes of Internet communications, thus affording individuals with their extensibility (Kellerman 2007). First among these communications modes are video calls, which obviously transmit the images of the callers themselves, but they further transmit images of some real space, visible in the background of the communicating parties. Videophones have been introduced repeatedly as of the 1960s, but have not been widely adopted until the wide adoption of broadband in general, and of smartphones connected to broadband transmission as of the 2000s, in particular.

The second mode of cyberspatial communications is verbal messaging, beyond the fixed-line audial telephone, which was introduced already in 1876, and has been gradually adopted in time and space since then (Kellerman 2006). The currently available rather numerous media for cyberspatial communications have been introduced and adopted as of the second half of the previous century, and particularly during the first decade of this century. These include e-mails (universally available as of 1994), faxes (commercially available as of 1964, and originally using fixed-line telephones), SMSs (Short Messaging Service) (as of 2000), chat messages transmitted through networking platforms (as of 2004), and Internet audial telephone calls through VoIP (as of 2003). This variety of interpersonal verbal communications technologies permit Internet subscribers to make use of both audial and written communications, side by side with their possible choice between online and delayed communications for written messages.

The Internet communications space is mostly interpersonal or shared by small groups such as most Whatsapp groups, though it may also be widely accessible to larger groups through other social networking systems, such as widely distributed blogs, or through networking platform, such as Myspace, Facebook, Twitter, and Usenets, or even through SMSs. Much of the contents of communications cyberspace is not recorded, and if it is recorded, then the contents is meant to be shared by the communicating parties only. However, so-called 'viral', swift and wide transmission of messages, transmitted through wide lists and groups, may cause a wide distribution of information, sometimes originally not been meant for wide distribution. Such viral distributions have brought about new social phenomena, such as shaming, and exposures of intimate pictures and information, side by side with stronger political awareness of the masses.

The two Internet categories of information and communications spaces are frequently interfolded, for example when website users send messages through the website itself to its owners, rather than separately through e-mail systems, or when e-mails and messages transmitted through social networking platforms include links to pictures, websites, and/or data. This interfolding and even fusing of the Internet information and communications spaces attest to the oneness of the Internet, at least from its usage perspective. However, each of the two cyberspace classes may frequently function independently of each other, for instance audial personal communications normally do not involve a simultaneous transmission of textual datasets.

2.4.3 Internet Screen-Space

Internet screen space constitute the visual interface between the Internet information and communications spaces and their users, and these digital spaces are displayed on computer and smartphone screens. Computer screens *per se* have already been explored from phenomenological (Introna and Ilharco 2006), as well as from ethological perspectives (Ash 2009), and we would like to add here a geographical framework for the understanding of the rather specific Internet screens. 'Online interaction is currently dominated by visual interfaces, rather than aural, tactile, or olfactory interfaces', and these digital spaces lead to the spatialization of non-spatial data (Zook et al. 2004, pp. 159–160; see also Fabrikant 2000). The comprehensive nature of the Internet as an informational and communications system implies that screen-spaces may consist of all possible visual presentation types: texts, pictures, maps, landscapes, and combinations among these elements.

Internet screen spaces, by their very nature, are not stable like printed or painted virtual spaces, and they may disappear by pre-programmed commands, or as a direct response to instant actions performed by users. Internet subscribers may use routinely and repetitively the same specific screen-spaces, such as their homepages, news services, and banking and shopping websites, and these repetitive uses present to the users pages with fixed structures and colors, but with some continuously contents changes. Thus, Internet users may find it difficult to cognize and eventually draw cognitive maps for these instantly appearing and disappearing virtual landscapes and informational screens (see Chap. 6 for discussion). More generally, Kwan (2001) noted in this regard, that for real space, space and its maps are two completely separate entities, whereas for Internet screen spaces, space and its maps may converge. Thus, 'cognitive communications cyberspaces are personally unique, and cannot be aggregated, whereas cognitive maps relating to a specific area may be compared and conclusions on a wider societal knowledge of an area drawn' (Kellerman 2014, p. 9). In telephone calls, notably in video calls, 'the virtual is imagined as a 'space' between participants, a computer-generated common ground which is neither actual in its location or coordinates, nor is it merely a conceptual abstraction, for it may be experienced 'as if' lived for given purposes' (Shields 2003, p. 49).

The use of the Internet, which implies the visual exposure of individuals to cyberspace, has involved simultaneous co-presence or telepresence of users in fixed physical and virtual spaces (see e.g., Kaufmann 2002, p. 28; Urry 2000, p. 71; Lévy 1998), and we will discuss this emerging routine of co-presence in detail in Chap. 5. Graham (2013) mentioned that cyberspace has been 'conceived of as both an ethereal dimension which is simultaneously infinite and everywhere… and as fixed in a distinct location' (p. 179), but he objected this view.

2.5 Image Spaces: Virtual Space, Cyberspace, the Internet and Internet Screen Space

In the discussions so far of the four classes of visual image space, namely virtual space, cyberspace, the Internet two spaces and Internet screen space, we have seen that each of them constitutes a geographical entity with some geographical, even if only metaphorical, qualities. We have further noted that virtual space is the widest entity, thus including within it both cyber and non-cyber spaces. Cyberspace, as the widest digital communications sphere, includes within it the Internet and its information and communications spaces, with Internet screen spaces constituting the visual interface of the Internet with is users. Internet screen-spaces enjoy a multifaceted nature: they are virtual, since they may visually present real space and material artifacts; they are cyberspatial, as they comprise a component of a digital communications medium; and finally they are Internet-based, because they serve as the visual interface of the Internet with its users. In the following chapters, we will move to discussions of real space dimensions and parameters that will be proposed for the interpretation and analysis of the Internet information and communications spaces, as well as for the Internet screen spaces.

2.6 Conclusion

In this chapter, we have presented image space as consisting of four visual classes: virtual space, cyberspace, the Internet two spaces, and Internet screen spaces. We interpreted virtual space as the visual presentations of real space and material artifacts in all forms, mainly on paper and through cyber, whereas cyberspace was viewed as being the specific subset of virtual space, with such presentations made through digital media, notably through the Internet. Thus, as such, the Internet constitutes a subset of cyberspace, which on its part is a subset of the wider virtual space. This differentiation has led us to the presentations of the even more specific Internet information, communications, and screen-spaces as subsets of the Internet.

Cyberspace has been spatially defined, in this chapter, from the perspectives of artificial reality, interactivity, and conceptual and metaphorical spaces, and it was shown to have a visual dimension through several media, including the Web and the communications platforms of the Internet, as transmitted via Internet screens. As a spatial experience, the exposure and use of cyberspace through the Internet involves co-presence in both cyber and real spaces, low cognitive mapping ability of individuals for cyberspatial landscapes, and personal exposure to the facilitation of communication through egalitarian and global interaction platforms.

References

Adams, C., & Warf, B. (1997). Introduction: Cyberspace and geographical space. *The Geographical Review, 87*, 139–145.

Adams, P. (1998). Network topologies and virtual place. *Annals of the Association of American Geographers, 88*, 88–106.

Adams, P. C. (1997). Cyberspace and virtual places. *The Geographical Review, 87*, 155–171.

Ash, J. (2009). Emerging spatialities of the screen: Video games and the reconfiguration of spatial awareness. *Environment and Planning A, 41*, 2105–2124.

Aumont, J. (1997). The Image (C. Pajackowska, Trans.). London: British Film Institute.

Batty, M. (1993). The geography of cyberspace. *Environment and Planning B, 20*, 615–616.

Batty, M. (1997). Virtual geography. *Futures, 29*, 337–352.

Benedikt, M. (1991). Cyberspace: Some proposals. In M. Benedikt (Ed.), *Cyberspace: First steps* (pp. 119–224). Cambridge, MA: MIT Press.

Couclelis, H. (1998). Worlds of Information: The geographic metaphor in the visualization of complex information. *Cartography and Geographic Information Systems, 25*, 209–220.

Crang, M., Crang, P., & May, J. (1999). Introduction. In M. Crang, P. Crang, & J. May (Eds.), *Virtual geographies: Bodies, space and relations* (pp. 1–13). London: Routledge.

Curry, M. R. (1998). *Digital places: Living with geographic information technologies*. London and New York: Routledge.

Dodge, M., & Kitchin, R. (2001). *Mapping cyberspace*. London: Routledge.

Doel, M., & Clarke, D. B. (2005). Emerging space and time: Moving pictures and motionless trips. *Journal of Historical Geography, 31*, 41–60.

Ettlinger, O. (2008). *The Architecture of virtual space*. Ljubljana: University of Ljubljana.

Fabrikant, S. I. (2000). Spatialized browsing in large scale data archives. *Transactions in GIS, 4*, 65–78.

Fabrikant, S. I., & Buttenfield, B. P. (2001). Formalizing semantic spaces for information access. *Annals of the Association of American Geographers, 91*, 263–280.

Farman, J. (2012). *Mobile interface theory: Embodied space and locative media*. New York: Routledge.

Gibson, W. (1984). *Neuromancer*. London: Gollancz.

Graham, M. (2013). Geography/Internet: Ethereal alternate dimensions of cyberspace or grounded augmented realities? *The Geographical Journal, 179*, 177–182.

Graham, S. (1998). The end of geography or the explosion of place? Conceptualizing space, place and information technology. *Progress in Human Geography, 22*, 165–185.

Graham, S. D. N. (2005). Software-sorted geographies. *Progress in Human Geography, 29*, 562–580.
Grosz, E. (2001). *Architecture from the outside: Essays on virtual and real space*. Cambridge, MA: MIT Press.
Hillis, K. (1999). *Digital sensations: Space, identity, and embodiment in virtual reality*. Minneapolis: University of Minnesota Press.
Introna, L., & Ilharco, F. M. (2006). On the meaning of screens: Towards a phenomenological account of screeness. *Human Studies, 29*, 57–76.
Jay, M. (1994). *Downcast eyes: The denigration of vision in Twentieth century French thought*. Berkeley: University of California Press.
Kaufmann, V. (2002). *Re-thinking mobility: Contemporary Sociology*. Aldershot: Ashgate.
Kellerman, A. (2002). *The internet on earth: A geography of information*. London: Wiley.
Kellerman, A. (2006). *Personal mobilities*. London and New York: Routledge.
Kellerman, A. (2007). Cyberspace classification and cognition: Information and communications cyberspaces. *Journal of Urban Technology, 14*, 5–32.
Kellerman, A. (2014). *The internet as second action space*. London and New York: Routledge.
Kellerman, A. (2016). Image Spaces and the Geography of Internet Screen-space. *Geojournal* 81 (forthcoming), DOI: 10.1007/s10708-015-9639-1.
Kinsley, S. (2014). The matter of 'virtual' geographies. *Progress in Human Geography, 38*, 364–384.
Kitchin, R. (1998a). *Cyberspace: The world in the wires*. Chichester: Wiley.
Kitchin, R. (1998b). Towards geographies of cyberspace. *Progress in Human Geography, 22*, 385–406.
Kwan, M.-P. (2001). Cyberspatial cognition and individual access to information: The behavioral foundation of cybergeography. *Environment and Planning B, 28*, 21–37.
Lakoff, G., & Johnson, M. (1980). *Metaphors we live by*. Chicago: The University of Chicago Press.
Lévy, P. (1998). *Becoming virtual: Reality in the digital age* (R. Bononno, Trans.). New York, London: Plenum Trade.
Light, J. S. (1999). From city space to cyberspace. In M. Crang, P. Crang, & J. May (Eds.), *Virtual geographies: Bodies, space and relations* (pp. 109–130). London: Routledge.
Mitchell, W. (1995). *City of bits: Space, place and the Infobahn*. Cambridge, MA: MIT Press.
Mizrach, S. (1996). Lost in cyberspace: A cultural geography of cyberspace. http://www2.fiu.edu/~mizrachs/lost-in-cyberspace.html.
Paradiso, M. (2011). Google and the Internet: A megaproject nesting within another megaproject. In S. Brunn (Ed.), *Engineering earth: The impacts of megaengineering projects* (Vol. 1, pp. 49–65). Dordrecht: Kluwer.
Petersson, D. (2005). Time and technology. *Environment and Planning D: Society and Space, 23*, 207–234.
Phillips, R. S. (1993). The language of images in geography. *Progress in Human Geography, 17*, 180–194.
Rose, G. (2003). On the need to ask how, exactly, is geography 'visual'? *Antipode, 35*, 212–221.
Schlottmann, A., & Miggelbrink, J. (2009). Visual geographies—an editorial. *Social Geography, 4*, 1–11.
Shields, R. (2003). *The virtual*. London and New York: Routledge.
Strate, L. (1999). The varieties of cyberspace: Problems in definition and delimitation. *Western Journal of Communication, 63*, 382–412.
Suler, J. (1999). Cyberspace as a dream world. http://users.rider.edu/~suler/psycyber/cybdream.html.
Thrift, N. (1996). New urban eras and old technological fears: Reconfiguring the goodwill of electronic things. *Urban Studies, 33*, 1463–1493.
Tranos, E., & Nijkamp, P. (2013). The death of distance revisited: Cyber-place, physical and relational proximities. *Journal of Regional Science, 53*, 855–873.

Tversky, B. (2000). Some ways that maps and diagrams communicate. In C. Freska, W. Brauer, C. Habel, & J. F. Wender (Eds.), *Spatial cognition II: Integrating abstract theories, empirical studies, formal methods, and practical applications* (pp. 72–79). Berlin: Springer.

Tversky, B. (2001). Spatial schemas in depictions. In M. Gattis (Ed.), *Spatial schemas and abstract thought* (pp. 79–112). Cambridge, MA: MIT Press.

Urry, J. (2000). *Sociology beyond Societies: Mobilities for the Twenty-first Century*. London: Routledge.

Wang, Y., Lai, P., & Sui, D. (2003). Mapping the internet using GIS: The death of distance hypothesis revisited. *Journal of Geographical Systems, 5*, 381–405.

Wilken, R. (2007). The haunting affect of place in the discourse of the virtual. *Ethics, Place and Environment, 10*, 49–63.

Wilson, M. I. (2001). Location, location, location: The geography of the dot.com problem. *Environment and Planning B: Planning and Design, 28*, 59–71.

Zook, M. A., & Graham, M. (2007). Mapping digiplace: Geocoded Internet data and the representation of place. *Environment and Planning B, 34*, 466–482.

Zook, M., Dodge, M., Aoyama, Y., & Townsend, A. (2004). New digital geographies: Information, communication, and place. In S. D. Brunn, S. L. Cutter, & J. W. Harrington (Eds.), *Geography and technology* (pp. 155–176). Dordrecht: Kluwer.

Chapter 3
Geographical Structures in the Internet

Abstract A basic element in the geographical study of terrestrial space is the ordering and division of this space, focusing mostly on the notions of ground, place, regions, and boundaries. This chapter will attempt to explore the possible extension of these concepts to Internet space, as well. More particularly, the possibility of viewing Internet screens as ground will be discussed, side by side with the potential application of other structural geographical notions to the Internet. Thus, the possible division of websites into regions will be elaborated, maybe via the suffix of their URL addresses, presenting countries or economic sectors. By the same token, the possible existence of boundaries in the most flexible and fluid Internet will be explored. The analysis of place over the Internet has been developed along the four perspectives proposed for real space: the neo-Marxist; the humanist; the feminist; and the performative.

Keywords Ground · Place · Regions · Boundaries

A basic dimension in the geographical study of terrestrial space is the structuring, ordering and internal division of specific pieces of space. This dimension of geographical study includes mainly the notions of ground or terrain, places, regions, and boundaries. In this chapter, we will attempt to explore the possible extension of these concepts for the interpretations of the cyberspatial Internet as a system, and for its components (information, communications, and screen spaces) in particular.

More specifically, we will examine, first, the possibility of viewing Internet screens as being similar, to that of ground for real space, in their basic spatial role for the cyberspatial Internet, as providers of background for visually presented information. Thus, we will treat screen spaces as being kind of a 'built' space, without the existence of 'natural' space or terrain on which it is constructed, as is the case for real space.

Following the discussion of ground, we will explore the potential application of several additional structural geographical notions for the Internet. First among these will be an exploration of the basic notion of 'place' within the context of the Internet, discussing the possibility of viewing websites as places, and in this regard

A. Kellerman, *Geographic Interpretations of the Internet*,
SpringerBriefs in Geography, DOI 10.1007/978-3-319-33804-0_3

we will examine in particular the possible application to the Internet of the four traditions that have emerged for the study of places in real space: Neo-Marxist, humanist, feminist and performative.

Following the discussion of places in the Internet, we will elaborate on the possible division of the Web into regions, via the suffixes of website URL (Uniform Resource Locator) addresses, which present countries and/or economic sectors for website domain registration. In addition, we will suggest interpreting the internal structures of websites as presenting a kind of division into regions, by website types, and as measured by their size, in form of their number of pages or screens.

Finally, we will explore the possible existence of boundaries within and between cyberspatial entities, in the rather virtual and thus most flexible Internet, as compared to the more solid real space, referring mainly to two aspects: free versus controlled access to the Internet, and the freedom of mobility of information that the Internet may facilitate.

The term 'geographical structures' is being used here, in the title of this chapter, as a kind of an 'umbrella' term for the four specific geographical concepts of ground, place, regions and boundaries, which jointly present the structural dimensions for geographic territories in real space and which may possibly do so also for cyberspace. However, it should be noted that this same term of 'geographical structures' is often used within a completely different context, namely in the study of the structures of organizations, as expressed through their functioning along geographical scalars, such as countries, regions, or cities (see e.g. Open/Learn 2015).

An equivalent and rather veteran term for geographical structures, which has been used often in geography, as well as in adjacent fields such as urban planning, is 'spatial structure', or more specifically 'urban spatial structure' (see e.g. Abler et al. 1971). We preferred the use of 'geographical structures' here, rather than spatial ones, in order to accentuate the word 'geographical', given our attempt here to assess the possible extension of terms and concepts which have been used originally for the geographical analysis of real space, also for the Internet.

3.1 Ground

It was already for Craine (2009) to suggest viewing the screen as equivalent to physical ground. As we noted already, there is however, a major difference between real space and cyberspace in this regard. Whereas real space consists of two layers, namely natural physical terrain and human-made space built on top of it, screen-space consists of a single human-made cyberspatial layer only. Also, by its very nature, there are no pre-existing container-like built spaces contained within Internet space, such as pre-existing built spaces for cities and regions in real space, in which the construction of new houses, roads etc. take place. Hence, spaces in cyberspace are created a posteriori only, through uniquely addressed Internet websites (Weinberger 2002, pp. 44–45).

We may assess screens by their information density, similarly to measures of spatial density for population and human-made artifacts in real space. In principle, therefore, the less textual information presented on screens the easier it becomes to read it and to 'digest' it. However, overusing this principle may yield an excessively large number of screens or pages per website, thus yielding longer surfing sessions by their users. Potential information density overload on screens for their viewers is often controlled through 'macro' screens coupled by 'micro' ones (Wroblewski 2004), or through the provision of links to other screens or websites.

Screen information overloading may be viewed as being similar to information overloading for individuals who happen to experience dense urban streets in real space, consisting of a variety of information inputs, mainly those of colorful signs, noises, cars, people and stores (Milgram 1970). Information overloading may emerge not only from condensed screens, but also from a continuous consulting of numerous websites. Such prolonged use of websites, or Internet information space, may emerge since Internet use via broadband connection is not measured anymore by duration, thus not involving high costs for prolonged use sessions (Rodríguez et al. 2015).

The 'ground' for Internet screens constitutes, in some way, the graphic background that appears on screens for the presentation of information within it. Thus, website designers have the equivalent role of both city planners and city governments in their double role of design and creation of the background for information presented on screens. However, this role for website designers has emerged gradually, and still back in Miller and Pupedis (2002) claimed that 'from a product design perspective, web-based spatial interfaces are still in an early developmental stage' (p. 119).

Screen designers base their work on the visual perspective of screen users, which is vertical, looking at the screen-information the way people see a city from a plane, unless pictures are shown on the screen and viewed by users either as frontal or profile images. This vertical angle of screen viewing is contrary to the viewing angle employed by city dwellers, who see and use urban public spaces from a rather horizontal perspective, with their bodies located within the viewed public sphere. Since users view information objects on screens from a vertical angle, the design of the normally small website screens has to take into account the overall visuality of the screen for its viewers, *vis-à-vis* the information presented on it.

Current information technologies permit website designers to make use of a wide variety of graphics for the design of both screen backgrounds and the information presented on screens on top of its background, including colors, patterns, icons, fonts, pictures, etc., all in attempt to create comfortable virtual environments for information reading. Furthermore, website designers may add an audial component to the background of websites, usually consisting of some proper music, thus creating a blend of visual and audial components for the background of the information presented on screens (see Kellerman 2014, pp. 21–24). Such a blend has to avoid, though, some possible audiovisual information overloading for screen viewers.

The sophisticated use of visual and audial elements for screen background is of special significance and importance for commercial websites. Such websites attempt to create attractive and inviting virtual environments for their users, in order for them to make extensive and repeating uses of the websites, and in order for them to purchase the services offered through the websites. The attractiveness of screen design has turned out to be of crucial importance for the contemporary tourism industry, which requires an extensive use of pictures and maps, and which has become mostly based on Internet marketing and Internet travel reserving. Thus, 'research in the hospitality and tourism field has demonstrated that website design and Internet marketing features contribute to effective delivery of messages, quality of products and services, and brand image' (Rodríguez et al. 2015, p. 303).

3.2 Place

The very existence of places on the Web and/or their experiencing by Internet users have been widely debated at the time (see Kwan 2001), but were still leading Wilken (2007, p. 54) to declare, 'that place is intrinsic to but largely suppressed in our understanding of CMC [computer-mediated communication] and the virtual'. Websites and their visual presentations on screens seem to lack the 'depth' of identity and history which places in real space can offer, but still, each website has its own identity, and if it is devoted to the presentation of a place in real space, then some of the flavor of the latter may be carried into cyberspace, as well.

The word 'place' probably constitutes 'one of the most multi-layered and multi-purpose words in our language' (Harvey 1993, p. 4), as manifested by its numerous and wide-ranging connotations (see e.g. OED 2015). The most relevant geographical meaning for place in daily linguistic use is probably: 'a particular part or region of space; a physical locality, a locale; a spot, a location' (OED 2015). For contemporary scientific geography this specific connotation for place in real space has been widely challenged, expanded and debated, notably regarding the human dimensions of places, the differences between the concepts of place and location, and the question of possible uniqueness which might be required from pieces of space in order for them to be identified as places (for a list of reviews see Seamon 2012). More specifically, places have been examined from the two-way perspective of individual and societal feelings and actions within places, on the one hand, and place meanings involved in those individual and societal feelings and actions, on the other (for a recent review see Agnew 2011).

The Internet, as the leading operational platform for human action within virtual cyberspace, lacks, by its very nature, the physical basis of places as prevalent in the real world. However, much of the diversified human activity over the Internet resembles patterns of human activities in real space, and growingly such activities have been moved there from physical space (Kellerman 2014). Thus, we will examine in this section the possibility of applying the notion of place to the Internet, and we will further discuss the potentially specific meanings of place in the Internet *vis-à-vis* the numerous ones offered for physical places.

We will begin our discussions with a brief elaboration on space, place, and the Internet, followed by specific discussions of cyberspace places along the four perspectives offered by Agnew (2011) for real-space places: neo-Marxist; humanist; feminist; and performative.

3.2.1 Space, Place, and the Internet

Numerous, and maybe most, websites, cannot be experienced as places. Such websites or pages within them may look very similar to each other, in terms of their structure and design, as well as in terms of their facilitation of user actions, so that they may differ from each other only by their contents. This possible similarity of form of websites may emerge even when design efforts may attempt to have them appear as unique. Such pages or websites present a rather generalized or somewhat nomothetic view of Internet cyberspace, notably since abstract space is nonexistent in or for cyberspace. However, other websites or their specific pages, may have, in numerous other cases, a unique, or idiographic, character in terms of their structure, and design, as well as in terms of their facilitation of user actions. Such websites, or some of their specific pages, being uniquely structured and designed Web pages, may potentially serve and be experienced, as virtual places in the Internet. Such virtual space experiencing, obviously depends on users. Virtual place feelings may emerge more frequently for websites devoted to real space places.

Regarding places in real space, Agnew (2011) noticed that 'new technologies—the container, the Internet, the cell phone—are making places obsolete' (p. 318). However, websites devoted to places, or virtual places devoted to real ones, may sustain and even amplify the meaning and identity of real places, since Internet information on places is easily accessible. The notion of place for real space has been associated with the nostalgic past, as compared with the seeming more progressive notion of location (Agnew 2011; see also Amin 2002), but such a distinction cannot be applied to the rather new Internet, in which the distinction between space and place is less relevant.

The interrelationships between space and place in the real world have been widely noted, such as in the claim that 'space provides the context for places but derives its meaning from particular places' (Relph 1976, p. 8). The view of real space places as entities that turn space into an active dimension (Feingold 2004), has additional significance for the virtual cyberspace, which has no particular existence per se, without websites and communications platforms located in it, and perceived as spaces. Real space places have been viewed as having a special role, among their numerous roles, for the production and dissemination of knowledge (Livingstone 2007), but for Internet places, or websites, information and knowledge provision is their only role, other than the possible facilitation of limited communications, in some special cases.

Places in real space have been viewed, at least from a phenomenological perspective, as lived space, thus requiring a population residing in them (Agnew 2011).

Cyberspace in general, and Internet websites in particular, obviously are not populated, and thus are not 'lived' through human residence in them. This lack of residential population in cyberspace has brought Bolter and Grusin (1999, p. 179) to view cyberspace as non-places, similarly to the non-places proposed for real space, such as airports. The notion of non-places for real space was suggested by Augé's (2000) who claimed that 'if a place can be defined as relational, historical and concerned with identity, then a space which cannot be defined as relational, or historical, or concerned with identity will be a non-place (pp. 77–78). Thus, for Bolter and Grusin (1999, p. 179), 'to Augé's list of nonplaces we would add cyberspace itself: the Internet and other manifestations of networked digital media. Cyberspace is not, as some assert, a parallel universe. It is not a place of escape from contemporary society, or indeed from the physical world. It is rather a non-place, with many of the same characteristics as other highly mediated nonplaces'. However, despite the seeming lack of 'depth' of identity and history for websites, as compared to places in real space, websites may possess their own identity through their design and functionalities, and, thus, be experienced as places by their users.

From yet another perspective, some websites may have little self-identity in their constitution of 'DigiPlaces', namely if they function as auxiliary tools for navigation in real space (Zook 2007). Other websites may now offer competing or alternative spaces or places for the performance of activities previously performed exclusively in real space, such as websites constituting stores and bank branches (Kellerman 2014). The users pf these latter websites may consider such websites as places, notably if they are designed similarly to the brick-and-mortar structures of such facilities in real space.

3.2.2 Neo-Marxist Perspectives for Internet Places

Lefebvre's (1991) neo-Marxist analysis of real space and its following interpretations (e.g. Harvey 1989; Merrifield 1993; Soja 1989; Chap. 1), suggest that 'abstract space', produced by capitalist forces, has overruled 'concrete space' (or places) of everyday life. As we noted in Chap. 1, this is expressed through individuals' spatial practices, through professional representations of space, such as by planners, as well as through artistic and portrayed spaces of representation (see also Agnew 2011; Kellerman 2014, pp. 31–35; Table 1.3). In some other, but somehow similar way, Castells (1998) distinguished between the emerging 'space of flows' and the rather veteran 'space of places', stating that 'the space of flows in the Information Age dominates the space of places of people's cultures' (p. 349).

These tensions between dominating space and dominated places in real space are irrelevant for cyberspace, since, as we noted already, cyberspace without Internet websites is practically nonexistent for Internet users. However, it is still for capitalist forces to bring about website ownerships by companies, and, thus, lead to the very construction of websites, as well as to their operation. These forces, then, determine the economic and social activities that take place in websites, maybe even in more absolute terms, as compared to activities performed in populated real space places. We can consider website users as being equivalent to residents and visitors of real places in terms of the activities that they carry out in websites, and in most cases, websites are open and accessible to all Internet users without charge. Thus, website users may represent a wide variety of people, as compared to those living in real places and those visiting them. Website users are conditioned only by knowledge of the language, or one of the languages, required for the use of any website, as the only requirement for website usage.

3.2.3 Humanist Agency-Based Aspects of Internet Places

The phenomenological-humanist approach to places relates to the materiality of places, to their residents and visitors, as well as to their spirit. Each of these dimensions may be interpreted through a variety of place aspects: interaction, identity, creation, intensification, realization, and release (Seamon 2012). Places, notably those of one's residence, such as homes, communities and towns, involve the evolution of feelings of personal attachments and experiences, or a 'sense of place', *á la* Relph (1976). Relph (1976) further noted the possible decline in such sense of place, when places have tended in recent times to undergo processes of standardization in their construction and landscaping, possibly leading to what he termed as 'placelessness'. In addition, Sack (1997, p. 16) noted that quick moving from one place to another, or the currently emerging fast personal mobilities, may constitute another possible source for a degraded experiencing of places.

Augé's (2000) notion of non-places is not synonymous with Relph's (1976) placelessness. Augé's (2000) non-places, which we noted before, accentuated more the lack of *social relations* within them, whereas Relph (1976) rather emphasized the *personal*, or rather experienced, lack of sense of place, which may eventually bring about his suggested 'placenessness'.

The very notion of sense of place coupled with the contemporary trends of its decline or even complete lacking, as far as places in real space are concerned, seem a priori irrelevant for users of virtual places. This is so since Internet users do not live in the virtual places, which they may access and use, and since they possibly may not experience them. However, Kwan (2001, p. 23) noted that still 'an individual's experience of using the Internet may engender a sense of 'place' or 'community'', thus providing some evidence that websites may evoke among their users a 'feeling of geography' and place, despite of the seemingly lack of topology, directionality, and boundaries in them. A frequent and orderly use of websites, notably those websites that do not change their structure and design too often, may imply some attachment to them and a possible emergence of usage experience, reflecting use habits by individuals. This might be the case notably when the use of some specific websites replaces equivalent visits of places in real space, such as stores.

3.2.4 *Feminist Interpretation for Internet Places*

Whereas the neo-Marxist approach accentuates the role of grand forces in the shaping of places, and the humanist approach views places from the perspective of their experiencing by individuals, the Feminist perspective views places as sites that facilitate the flows of social relations (see e.g. Massey 1994; McDowell 1993; Moss and Falconer Al-Hindi 2008). Thus, according to the feminist view, the living and experiencing of places has foremost a sectoral and gender pattern. ‘People are everywhere conceptualizing and acting on different spatialities (‘global sense of place’)….And the particularity of place is…constructed not by placing boundaries around it and defining its identity through counterposition to the other which lies beyond, but precisely (in part) through its specificity of the mix of links and interconnections *to* that ‘beyond’. Places viewed this way are open and porous’ (Massey 1994, pp. 4–5).

This perspective may seem irrelevant for Internet websites, because websites do not enjoy a residential population that could possibly maintain any social relations within them. However, the feminist perspective might still be relevant for the Internet, concerning the very use of Internet websites, and this may be the case for two dimensions. First, the very access to the Internet system might not be equal along gender (see Chap. 1), as well as along other social and demographic sectors, thus bringing about some ‘digital gap’. Second, the actual patterns of choice for specific websites and their use may differ along gender, as well as along other social sectors.

Differences along gender may emerge, for example, in the frequency and use habits of websites specializing in online shopping, notably in those specializing in the sale of clothing, in some similarity to gender differences in the use of real space shopping centers. A survey among Internet users in the US indicated that male preferences were for entertainment and leisure websites, whereas female ones focused primarily on interpersonal communications and educational assistance (Weiser 2000). Surveys among Chinese and British students as Internet users revealed similarly that males played more computer games than women did, but in contrary to the American survey, conducted seven years earlier, the Chinese and British results showed that men used e-mail and chats more than women did (Li and Kirkup 2007).

3.2.5 *Performative Interpretation for Internet Places*

From a performative perspective, developed mainly by Thrift (1999), real space places constitute ‘associational’ entities or a kind of projects, in the sense that places are continuously in the making, and thus they are always incomplete, and requiring additional action and change by their ‘actants’. From a gender perspective, Butler (1990) suggested the *gender performativity*, which does not focus on change but rather on the stratification of performativity, so that permanent social customs in a given place may conceal personal gender-based activities. In addition to these two local perspectives, in a globalized world places may turn into ‘traces of movement, speed and circulation' (Thrift 1996, p. 289), with both local and external sources and forces for the development of idiosyncratic place identities (see Kellerman 2002, pp. 40–41).

Thrift's performative approach can be easily applied to the interpretation of most Internet websites, the contents and design of which are normally under frequent or continuous updating by their owners and designers, respectively. Users may also bring about changes in websites, notably in Web 2.0 social networking platforms, where the contents of websites is also under continuous change by their users. Still, however, since people do not reside in websites, their association with them, via their performance within them, is rather restricted in terms of their personal involvement with them, as compared to their involvement in real space places.

In summary, then, the four perspectives that were proposed for the interpretation of real space places do not necessarily constitute four distinct alternatives for real space place interpretation, and they may rather be seen as complementing each other, with each of them accentuating another force and meaning for places. This is true also regarding their relevance in some ways for virtual places, as well. Thus, there are capitalist *forces* that lead the operation of places and websites (the Neo-Marxist approach); places are *experienced* by their residents and possibly also by website users (the humanist perspective); *social relations* emerge within them, as well as with regard to website access and use (the feminist interpretation); and, finally, a variety of *performances* is carried out within them (the performative approach). The ownership of websites, and their business objectives, may be reflected in the design of a website and its operations, thus having a direct impact on the website experiencing by its users, and users' performances within it. However, the facilitation of access to a website and the identity of its users might be determined by wider societal structures.

3.3 Regions

'*Region* and *place* are multifarious concepts' (Smith 1996, p. 189), and we noted this multiplicity already with regard to places. However, generally, 'a *region* is a subdivision of something larger, more extensive' (Smith 1996, p. 189). Thus, regions may normally refer to formal and informal divisions of a geographical territory, to parts of the human body, or to areas or fields of human activity or thought (Oxford Dictionaries 2015). The notion of regions in the Internet may obviously refer to the presentation of real space regions in Internet websites (see e.g. Terlouw 2011). However, in our following brief discussion on regions in the Internet, we will rather refer to the possible existence of regions within the cyberspatial Internet itself.

If Internet screens are considered as ground or territory, as we did earlier in this chapter, then it is normally impossible to divide such screens into regions of information presentation, because of the full flexibility facilitated by the Web for patterns and styles of information presentations, so that screens may present changing idiosyncratic designs.

From yet another perspective, looking at the Web at large, in its constitution of a grand information system consisting of close to one billion websites, we can see that this system is clearly unorganized along any systematic scalar or regional structures other than domain names. The basic real-world geographical scale for the internal division of countries, ranging from the local through the regional to the national, is irrelevant for the internal division or structure of the Web at large, nor for specific websites or portals. In the early days of the Internet, some still believed that the Internet should be organized along regions. 'We should design regions in cyberspace so that people implicitly sense what is expected and what is appropriate. In this respect, designers of virtual communities can learn a great deal from architects' (Bruckman 1996). However, the Internet has rather developed in an unorganized way, thus lacking any 'contents regions'. The introduction of search engines for the search of websites through keywords has completely nullified any benefit for users from any potential regional divisions or classifications of websites and cyberspatial information.

It is still possible, though, to identify two scalars of regional division of Web information, one relating to the internal structure of information within websites, and the other one relating to the organization of websites within the global system of the Internet. Within websites, the size and internal structure of websites might be considered as a kind of regional subdivision, with 'regional' in this case, not carrying a geographical connotation. These two website dimensions of size and structure can be measured by the number of pages per website, as well as by the internal organizational structure of information presented through them. Thus, websites may range from single-page ones through multi-heading and hierarchical ones to portals. Portals are divided, in many cases, into classes and subclasses of information, thus usually including multiple hypertext links within them, leading to numerous other, and mostly completely separate, websites.

As for the organization of websites within the global system of the Internet, the system-wide class divisions of domains/websites is by their suffixes, which relate to two 'regional' classifications. The first one is by type of activity (gTLDs, generic Top-Level Domains), such as commerce ('co' or 'com'), education ('ac' or 'edu'), organization ('org'), information ('in'), and government ('gov'). The second system-wide classification of domains is by the country of their registration (ccTLDs, country code Top-Level Domains), applying to all non-American domains, and using the international two-letter code for each country. The first classification is again 'regional' in a rather metaphorical sense, whereas the latter one is of course, a clear geographical division, reflecting 'geographies of participation' in cyberspatial information production (Graham et al. 2015).

It should be noted, though, that these two classifications by address suffixes, are used for the purposes of the very management of the Internet. However, from the perspective of Internet users, these two classifications, of activity type and nationality of registration, carry no significance, since websites are not structured or ordered within the Web along their type, neither by organizational activity nor by country. Users rather search the system through keywords, and these searches by individual users within the system are independent of any of the two domain codes.

Thus, one cannot use standard search engines for the search of groups of websites, all of which related to the same searched keywords, but rather the search results are presented as lists of separate and single websites. In addition, standard search engines will not present search results by lists of websites classified separately along their country codes of their URL addresses.

The global regional geography of domain registration in 2015 has been still typified by a heavy American dominance, with some 56.1 percent of the domains worldwide registered in the US, followed by much more modest shares for Germany (6.5 %), Canada (5.8 %), and China (4.3 %) (DomainState 2015). The American suffix '.com' has turned over the years into the most dominant suffix code for commercial Internet addresses worldwide, with 78.4 % of all the Internet domains being '.com' in 2015. This tendency presents registrations in the US for website addresses of commercial companies, even for those whose physical location was in effect in other countries.

In addition to the American dominance of the global domain registration system through the '.co' suffix, some 68.4 % of all types of websites were hosted in servers located in the US in 2015 (Webhosting.info 2015). These statistics present a rather heavy American dominance in the geography of the Internet, notably in cyberspatial information production and transmission, though it is now over 30 years since the introduction of the Internet in the US, and with Internet consumption now diffused globally, though still unequally (see Wilson et al. 2013; Chap. 1).

Another regional division of real space, of a rather micro nature, is the division of both urban and rural spaces into land parcels or lots, owned by individuals, companies and governments. Pieces of land owned personally by individuals may create for them feelings of territoriality. Feelings of territoriality may apply also to invisible bubbles of personally unowned territories, such as seating places, or personal space around one's body (see e.g. Gold 1980). Such territoriality may also be relevant for personal webpages or websites, which are pieces of the cyberspatial Internet, owned or operated by private people. Internet territoriality was further relevant at the early phases of the Internet with regard to desirable domain names, which were sold among companies (see Wilson 2001). This trend lost much of its value with the growing use of keywords through search engines rather than direct typing of Internet addresses. In the communications space of the Internet, the emergence of open social networks has implied, among other things, a decline in the privacy of subscribers, or in their bubble territory, notably since free expression, including personal shaming, has become a permitted norm in networks such as Facebook and Twitter.

3.4 Boundaries

In real space, physical and signified international borders or barriers have been proposed and have been in existence since early Biblical times (Burghardt 1996), and such boundaries have prevented, or just controlled, cross-border flows. In addition, there have existed signified or hidden domestic boundaries mainly within cities, prohibiting or controlling access or entrance to specific places and spaces. Thus, the study of boundaries *and* the Internet may refer to the blurring and normally even the complete disappearance of international borders as far as access and use of websites and digital communications are concerned, as is the case for numerous countries in the free world. This disappearance of borders in the transmission of Internet information has not implied similar processes in real space, so that international boundaries are still clearly marked in real space (see e.g. Everard 2000).

Specifically regarding Internet interpersonal interactions, the cross-border information flows through the Internet have provided for 'the potential for communication irrespective of intervening distance or national borders [which] facilitates the growth of communities on the basis of interest or outlook, rather than geographical proximity' (Collyer 2003, p. 348). However, while individuals these days may access websites from all over the world for their diversified information needs, most people still tend to socially communicate with friends and family located nearby in physical space, rather than being involved in global social networks (Rainie and Wellman 2012, pp. 13, 130–131; Kellerman 2014). Furthermore, it was shown repeatedly that even among migrants, who should have potentially tie with fellows living in both their country of origin and their country of resettlement, Internet contacts are preferred within their current country of residence (see the review by Collyer 2003). Thus, international boundaries in physical space still have some significance for the overall worldwide patterns of interpersonal communications over the Internet.

The question of boundaries *within* the Internet is different from that of boundaries *and* the Internet. The Web, in principle at least, provides 'doors' for entering 'other' spaces, through links among websites, and the marking of these links on website pages does not require permission by website 'owners' or creators for the very establishment of such links to them by other websites (Weinberger 2002, pp. 52–53). Obviously, inter-website linking can and is made without regard of international boundaries. Still, however, entering some websites may require registration and/or payment, membership, minimum age, or knowledge of some language, whereas for some other websites, access through linking or directly might be denied altogether by governmental censorship (Warf 2013).

The Web 2.0 system, consisting of the social networking platforms, may permit completely free communications among all subscribers of networks, such as Facebook and Twitter, something that has applied also to e-mail interaction. We noted already the preference by network subscribers to interact mainly with individuals located nearby. However, communications patterns may also reflect barriers representing cultural or religious norms that prevent free communications, for instance between women and men. Cultural/religious censorships may imply a reflection of social class prevailing in real space through use patterns of the Internet, with social groups who do not obey to cultural restrictions in any national society, enjoying higher freedom of communications, as well as wider choices of information sources.

Furthermore, political governmental actions of censorships may prevent international Internet communications, as has been the case, for example, with regard to the use of Facebook in China (see Warf 2013). Such censorships may involve daily constraints and hardships for business, as well as for intellectual and social interactions. If certain groups of people, such as government workers, are exempt from some or all censorships, then, once again, virtual space may reflect social classes that exist in real space.

The setting of barriers for the seemingly borderless international communications in cyberspace can be considered as equivalent to the establishment of a country's international borders in physical space. In both cases, some people may attempt to cross illegally these spatial or cyberspatial borders, and in both cases border crossers may be subjected to severe punishment. Thus, in countries that control the international flows of information, these flows might have a similar status to cross-border flows of people and commodities. However, in countries that permit free cross-border flows of information, such freedom turns out to be much wider than that of the equivalent flows of people and commodities, since the latter may require some licensing (through passports and visas for people, and customs and licensing for commodities), and these latter flows are always controlled.

3.5 Conclusion

In this chapter, we explored the possible extension of the structuring, ordering and internal division of specific pieces of real space for some possible interpretations of cyberspatial Internet spaces. We focused in this regard on the notions of ground or terrain, places, regions, and boundaries.

Screens may be viewed as being equivalent to physical ground. However, whereas real space consists of two layers, namely natural physical terrain and human-made space built on top of it, screen-space consists of a single human-made cyberspatial layer only, and it may, thus, be considered as ground a posteriori only. It is possible to assess screens by their information density, similarly to measures of spatial density for residential population and human-made artifacts in real space. Furthermore, screen information overloading for Internet users may be viewed as being similar to information overloading for urbanites experiencing dense urban environments.

The 'ground' for Internet screens constitutes, specifically, the graphic background that appears on screens for the presentation of information within it. Website designers take a double role, equivalent to both city planners and city governments, in their responsibility for the design and creation of the background for information presented on screens. Users view information objects on screens from a vertical perspective, so that the design of website screens has to take into account the overall visuality of the screen. Sophisticated uses of visual and audial elements for screen background are of special significance and importance for commercial websites, notably in the tourism industry, which attempt to create attractive and inviting virtual environments for their users.

Websites, or some of their specific pages, may potentially serve as virtual places in the Internet. The major difference between real space places and virtual ones is that the latter are not populated. However, the growing use of virtual places or Internet websites has turned their users, at least in some restricted sense, into kind of website residents that act and feel similarly to residents of real space places. Furthermore, the growing use of websites is partially at the expense of action that used to take place in real space places. This place replacement between the two spaces may weaken the forces, feelings, relations and performance attributed to places in real space in favor of the rather virtual websites.

It is possible to apply to virtual places the four contemporary geographical interpretations proposed for real space places, all of which focus foremost on their residential population. First, there are capitalist forces that produce websites and there are users-actors for activities that take place in them (the neo-Marxist approach). Second, website users may experience place-related feelings under some circumstances (the humanist approach). Third, access to websites and their use involve social relations, through societal sectoral gaps in levels of access to websites and in their use (the feminist approach). Fourth, websites and networking platforms are typified by continuous change performance regarding the contents of websites (the performative approach).

It is normally impossible to divide individual screens, perceived as ground, into regions of information presentation. In addition, and at the macro level, the whole Web, which consists of millions of websites, is clearly unorganized along any systematic scalar or regional structures other than domain names. However, regions may still be identified both within websites and within the Web at large. Within websites, the size, measured by the number of screens, and the internal structure of websites, notably of portals, might be considered as a kind of regional subdivision, with 'regional' in this case, not carrying a geographical connotation. The system in general is divided along the two suffixes of the URL domain addresses for websites, namely by information or organization type of domain owners, and by country of domain registration. Both classifications exhibit heavy American dominance in the production side of Internet information.

International boundaries in physical space still have some significance for the overall patterns of interpersonal communications over the Internet, as individuals prefer to communicate with fellows located close by. Interpersonal communications might be sanctioned by cultural and religious norms, as well as by governmental censorship, preventing or controlling international communications. Websites are normally open for full or partial free use, by domestic, as well as by international, users. Websites are further interconnected with each other through links that are proposed on their pages. Such links may direct users to websites located all over the world. Thus, information may flow freely across international borders where permitted, as compared to the flows of people and commodities that are still controlled by all countries or unions of countries, such as the EU.

In summary then, it is possible to extend some basic notions pertaining to the structuring of real space for the structuring of cyberspace via the Internet and its components, and in numerous ways. Internet screens may act as ground, notably so for screen background. In addition, some websites may be viewed and experienced as places, through activities taking place in them, as well as through their experiencing. Websites internally, and the Web in general, may be divided into kinds of regions, and Finally, international boundaries are still of significance for Internet communications, as well as for access to Web information.

References

Abler, R., Adams, J. S., & Gould, P. (1971). *Spatial organization: The geographer's view of the world*. Englewood Cliffs NJ: Prentice-Hall.

Agnew, J. A. (2011). Space and place. In J. A. Agnew & D. N. Livingstone (Eds.), *The SAGE handbook of geographical knowledge* (pp. 316–360). London: SAGE.

Amin, A. (2002). Spatialities of globalization. *Environment and Planning A, 34*, 385–399.

Augé, M. (2000). *Non-places: Introduction to an anthropology of supermodernity* (J. Howe Trans.). London: Verso.

Bolter, J. D., & Grusin, R. (1999). *Remediation: Understanding new media*. Cambridge, MA: MIT Press.

Bruckman, A. (1996). Finding one's own in cyberspace. Technology Review Magazine, January. http://www.cc.gatech.edu/~asb/papers/tr-finding-ones-own.pdf.

Burghardt, A. F. (1996). Boundaries: Setting limits to political areas. In C. Earle, K. Mathewson, & M. S. Kenzer (Eds.), *Concepts in human geography* (pp. 213–230). Lanham, MD: Rowman and Littlefield.

Butler, J. (1990). *Gender trouble: Feminism and the subversion of identity*. New York: Routledge.

Castells, M. (1998). *End of millennium*. Oxford: Blackwell.

Collyer, M. (2003). Are there national borders in cyberspace? *Geography, 88*, 348–356.

Craine, J. (2009). Virtualizing Los Angeles: Pierre Levy, The Shield, and http://theshieldrap.proboard45.com/. GeoJournal, 74, 235–243.

DomainState (2015). Domain name registrar stats. http://www.domainstate.com/registrar-stats.html.

Everard, J. (2000). *Virtual states: The internet and the boundaries of the nation-state*. London: Routledge.

Feingold, M. (2004). *The newtonian moment: Isaac newton and the making of modern culture*. New York: Oxford University Press.

Gold, J. R. (1980). *An introduction to behavioural geography*. Oxford: Oxford University Press.

Graham, M., de Sabbata, S., & Zook, M. A. (2015). Towards a study of information geographies: (im)mutable augmentations and a mapping of the geographies of information. *Geo: Geography and Environment, 2*, 88–105.

Harvey, D. (1989). *The condition of postmodernity*. Oxford: Blackwell.

Harvey, D. (1993). From space to place and back again: Reflections on the condition of postmodernity. In J. Bird, B. Curtis, T. Putnaman, G. Robertson, & L. Tickner (Eds.), *Mapping the futures: Local cultures, global change* (pp. 3–29). London: Routledge.

Kellerman, A. (2002). *The Internet on earth: A geography of information*. London, New York: Wiley.

Kellerman, A. (2014). *The Internet as second action space*. London, New York: Routledge.

Kwan, M.-P. (2001). Cyberspatial cognition and individual access to information: The behavioral foundation of cybergeography. *Environment and Planning B, 28*, 21–37.

Lefebvre, H. (1991). The production of space. In D. Nicholson-Smith (Trans.). Oxford: Basil Blackwell.

Li, N., & Kirkup, G. (2007). Gender and cultural differences in Internet use: A study of China and the UK. *Computers & Education, 48*, 301–317.

Livingstone, D. N. (2007). Science, site and speech: Scientific knowledge and the spaces of rhetoric. *History of the Human Sciences, 20*, 71–98.

Massey, D. (1994). *Space, place, and gender*. Minneapolis: University of Minnesota Press.
McDowell, (1993). Space, place and gender relations: Part I. Feminist empiricism and the geography of social relations. *Progress in Human Geography, 17*, 157–179.
Merrifield, A. (1993). Place and space: A Lefebvrian reconciliation. *Transactions of the British Institute of Geographers, 18*, 516–531.
Milgram, S. (1970). The experience of living in cities. *Science, 167*, 1461–1468.
Miller, S., & Pupedis, G. (2002). Spatial interface design for the web—A question of usability. *Cartography, 31*, 119–134.
Moss, P., & Falconer Al-Hindi, K. (Eds.). (2008). *Feminisms in geography: Rethinking space, place and knowledges*. Lanham, MD: Rowman and Littlefield.
OED (Oxford English Dictionary) (2015). Place. http://www.oed.com/view/Entry/144864?rskey=3Vv78q&result=1#eid.
Open/Learn (2015). Organizations and management accounting. The Open University. http://www.open.edu/openlearn/money-management/organisations-and-management-accounting/content-section-3.3.
Oxford Dictionaries (2015). Region. http://www.oxforddictionaries.com/definition/english/region.
Rainie, L., & Wellman, B. (2012). *Networked: The new social operating system*. Cambridge, MA: MIT Press.
Relph, E. (1976). *Place and placelessness*. London: Pion.
Rodríguez-Molina, M. A., Frías-Jamilena, D. M., & Castañeda-García, J. A. (2015). The contribution of website design to the generation of tourist destination image: The moderating effect of involvement. *Tourism Management, 47*, 303–317.
Sack, R. D. (1997). *Homo geographicus*. Baltimore: Johns Hopkins University Press.
Seamon, D. (2012). Place, place identity, and phenomenology: A triadic interpretation based on J.G. Bennet's systematics. In H. Casakin & F. Bernardo (Eds.), *The role of place identity in the perception, understanding, and design of built environments* (pp. 3–21). Oak Park, IL: Bentham Science Publishers.
Smith, J. M. (1996). Ramifications of region and senses of place. In C. Earle, K. Mathewson, & M. S. Kenzer (Eds.), *Concepts in human geography* (pp. 189–211). Lanham, MD: Rowman and Littlefield.
Soja, E. W. (1989). *Postmodern geographies: The reassertion of space in critical social theory*. London: Verso.
Terlouw, K. (2011). The geography of regional websites: Regional representations and regional structure. *Geoforum, 42*, 578–591.
Thrift, N. (1996). *Spatial formations*. London: Sage.
Thrift, N. (1999). Steps to an ecology of place. In D. Massey, J. Allen, & P. Sarre (Eds.), *Human Geography today* (pp. 295–321). Cambridge: Polity.
Warf, B. (2013). *Global geographies of the Internet*. Dordrecht: Springer.
Webhosting.info (2015). Domain statistics. http://www.webhosting.info/domain-names/domain-statistics;jsessionid=CA85BA296E158ADABECCFB86689BB182.
Weinberger, D. (2002). *Small pieces loosely joined {a unified theory of the web}*. Cambridge, MA: Perseus.
Weiser, E. B. (2000). Gender differences in Internet use patterns and Internet application preferences: A two-sample comparison. *CyberPsychology & Behavior, 3*, 167–178.
Wilken, R. (2007). The haunting affect of place in the discourse of the virtual. *Ethics, Place and Environment, 10*, 49–63.
Wilson, M. I. (2001). Location, location, location: The geography of the dot.com problem. *Environment and Planning B: Planning and Design, 28*, 59–71.
Wilson, M. I., Kellerman, A., & Corey, K. E. (2013). *Global information society: Knowledge, mobility and technology*. Lanham, MD: Rowman and Littlefield.
Wroblewski, L. (2004). Visual simplicity vs. information density. LUKEW. http://www.lukew.com/ff/entry.asp?15.
Zook, M. A. (2007). Mapping DigiPlace: Geocoded Internet data and the representation of place. *Environment and Planning B: Planning and Design, 34*, 466–482.

Chapter 4
Distance in the Internet

Abstract Distance has been considered as a primal geographical notion for physical space, possibly with some declining importance in the information age. This view will, first, be elaborated on, followed by specific discussions on the possible extension of the notions of distance, distance decay, distanciation, and proximity, for the analysis of the Internet. In Internet surfing, access duration increases with growing physical distance to hosting servers. Such servers may be viewed as centers, with users located around them along increasing physical distance/access time. In website searches via search engines, the order of search results presented on Internet screens is of special significance, since users prefer the first result, which serves, therefore, as a center on the Internet screen, with declining uses of lower ranked results. From yet another dimension, communications and networking permit contacts among Internet users without regard to distance. Still, users, as centers, keep more Internet ties with physically closer people.

Keywords Distance · Distance decay · Distanciation · Proximity

4.1 Introduction

Distance constitutes a primal geographical notion for the study and interpretation of physical space. At least potentially, and as has been argued widely, it should have had a declining importance in the information age, given the contemporary speedy transmissions of information. However, as we will see along this chapter, distance presents a variety of significances for the Internet, for both its information and communications classes.

Distance was traditionally defined as 'the length of the space between two points' (OED 2015a). This definition assumes that space constitutes the measure for distance in real space. One of our major concerns here will be to check whether cyberspace could be counted as equivalent to real space, for the very existence, as well as for the measurement of virtual distance. The notion of relative space in geography is based on the distance that separates among objects and entities in

A. Kellerman, *Geographic Interpretations of the Internet*,
SpringerBriefs in Geography, DOI 10.1007/978-3-319-33804-0_4

physical space, but cyberspace was argued to constitute neither absolute nor relative space (Wang et al. 2003, and we will discuss the special status of cyberspace, as compared to real space in Chap. 7).

A second facet of distance *and* the Internet is the relationships between the Internet and urban and regional developments, taking place in physical space. We will not examine this dimension in detail here, and it will suffice to note, for example, the possibility of population growth in remote cities, based on the availability of broadband access there to the Internet in general, and to online shopping in particular (see e.g., Pons-Novell and Viladecans-Marsal 2006).

A third interpretation for distance in the use of the Internet is the physical access of users to the Internet, or the real distance that users have to pass, through walking or traveling, in order for them to reach any kind of stations with Internet connections, an issue discussed elsewhere (Yu and Shaw 2008; Kellerman 2014; Chap. 1). This distance may also be expressed and measured by the levels of spread of Internet infrastructures, such as that of wide bandwidth, and people's access to these infrastructures. The notion of distance to the Internet, as a measure for users' access to the Internet, may, thus, reflect the digital gaps among individuals, social sectors and regions, in their ability to access the Internet (Chap. 1).

Our interest here, in similarity to our focus in the previous chapter, is rather on distance *within* the Internet itself, rather than on distance *and* the Internet, which we briefly outlined in the previous paragraphs. The term distance for both physical and virtual spaces, including distances within the Internet, refers, as we will see, specifically to the measured separations between points in space. It may further refer to a set of some additional specific concepts, which have been derived directly from the general concept of distance. Such concepts are distance decay, distanciation, and proximity. We will begin our elaborations below by discussing, first, the possible extension of the primal and general concept of distance to cyberspace. This discussion of distance in the Internet will be followed by separate discussions of the more specific concepts of distance decay, distanciation and proximity, with the same objective as in the previous chapter, namely trying to see whether these concepts, which were developed originally for the study of real space, may be applied for the Internet, as well.

4.2 Distance

The concept of distance was declared for cyberspace use, in the 1990s, 'as the concept on which modern geography was built' (Couclelis 1996, p. 387). This line of thought has attempted to extend for cyberspace the traditional views of distance for real space, but it was contested at the same time by a quite provocative view, offered in the book *The Death of Distance* (Cairncross 1997). This alternative view of distance and the Internet claimed for a possible, and most significant, contemporary decline in the importance of distance among physical places, as well as among people, because of the development of telecommunications (see also Nashleanas 2011). This notion of a contemporary decline in the significance of distance in real space was extended also for distance within cyberspace: 'there is no geographical landmark or physical movement in 'cyberspace' for telling either distance or orientation' (Kwan 2001, p. 23). We will examine the issue of the significance of measured distance *in* physical space *for* cyberspace in our later discussion in this chapter focusing on distance decay, and elaborating on the travel speeds of Internet information.

Cyberspace users may still experience a sense of distance despite the seeming lack of and irrelevance of measured physical distance within the virtual Internet, at least for its routine users. Weinberger (2002, p. 45) noted in this respect that 'distance on the Web is measured by links', and 'links are all that holds the Web together; without links, there is no Web' (p. 54, see also Wang et al. 2003). Thus, distances over the Internet may be measured by the number of clicks which users may be required to make in order for them to reach specific pages within websites, or the number of clicks needed in order for them to reach other websites, assuming that proper links are provided on website pages (see also Ash 2009, pp. 2113–4). Wang et al. (2003) claimed in their study of websites of American universities that there is some relationship between the numbers of clicks required to reach the websites of other universities from any university website, on the one hand, and the physical distance in real space among the institutes which own these websites, on the other.

This same principle of distance as expressed by the number of clicks applies also for the communications class of the Internet, namely for e-mailing, and even more so for social networking. Communications distance may be expressed by the number of clicks needed by subscribers in order for them to reach a certain individual, so that the number clicks constitutes a measure of distance among people in cyberspace.

Generally then, the number of clicks amounts to the time and effort applied to Internet search, surfing, use, and communicating, and this is similar to the idea of time and effort involved in real space travel. As of yet, the cyberspatial distance as measured by the number of clicks, has not matured into a formal metric, similarly to distance metrics employed for real space. In other words, so far, Internet users normally do not compare the number of clicks they have to make for specific searches, nor do they check the number of clicks made for surfing sessions, or for searches for people, but such a tendency may emerge in the future.

4.3 Distance Decay

Distance decay patterns may emerge within the Internet for three of its uses: in surfing sessions, in search sessions, and in social communications. Thus, the first two cases apply to the Internet information space, whereas the third one applies to its communications space. The first distance decay pattern, occurring in surfing for information, is experienced in the duration of users' access to websites. This distance decay pattern may apply both to users who attempt to access websites through search engines, as well as to those who surf directly to some targeted websites. The access durations to websites may increase with growing physical distances from users' computers or smartphones to the hosting servers for the contacted websites. Thus, the contacted hosting servers may be viewed as centers, with users located around them along increasing physical distances, with the latter coupled growing access times.

The second type of distance decay applies also to information surfing, but this time only to searches for desired websites through search engines. The specific distance decay pattern for search sessions has a completely different setting, as compared to that of access distance for surfing sessions. It rather refers to the structure of the Internet screens that present the search results and distances within it. The order of these search results as presented on Internet screens is of special significance, since users tend to access the first suggested result that appears on the top of the screen. This result serves, therefore, as a center for the Internet results screen, with declining attention and possible access by users to results ranking in lower orders. Thus, the presentation of information on search screens involves a virtual distance decay pattern.

The third type of distance decay in the Internet is in social communications via e-mail and social networking, and it refers to distance decay in real space. The cyberspatial interactions by subscribers to called counterparts may reflect distance decays from their fixed physical locations, normally their homes, to those of the called parties. In other words, subscribers prefer to be in cyberspatial touch with people who are located close to them in real space. Thus, distance decay patterns in the virtual communications space reflect social distance decays in real space.

Our following detailed discussions of these three types of distance decay in cyberspace will begin with some rather general introductory remarks on distance decay in real space. We will then move to an elaboration on distance decay patterns within the Web, i.e. in the use of websites through users' surfing to specific websites (pattern one as above), and our focus in this discussion will be on distance decay patterns in Internet information flows. Following this discussion of the first expression of distance decay on the Web, we will discuss the use of search engines that permit the finding of specific websites, which may fully fit some specific keywords typed by users (pattern two as above). Our discussion on this type of distance decay will refer, first, to centrality, navigation, and distance in the Internet in general from the users' perspective, and we will then apply these notions to an examination of the specific case of distance decay in the use of Internet search engines. The last subsection on distance decay will highlight distance decay patterns in the communications class of the Internet, namely in e-mail and social networking applications (pattern three as above).

4.3.1 *Distance Decay in Real Space*

The concept of decay for some values along growing distance from a center has surely been one of the earliest notions developing in modern geography. It dates back to the late 18th century, when Von Thünen formulated his classical crop and intensity theories (see e.g., Kellerman 1983, 1989a, b). Thus, the concept of distance decay was developed originally for agricultural land-use densities, land costs and incomes from land located around an urban center, or the market for the agricultural products grown around it. The concept was extended later on for urban land values and densities, as well (e.g., Alonso 1964). Thus, distance decay patterns and functions have normally been identified for growing distances from cities or from city centers.

Distance decay patterns for conditions in real space constitute a striking expression of Tobler's 'first law of geography' (TFL), defined as 'everything is related to everything else, but near things are more related than distant things' (Tobler 1970, p. 236; see also Sui 2004). The possible extension of the notion of distance decay for the Internet has, therefore, to identify the centers from which distances are to be measured, side by side with the identification of the things or values that may decay from these virtual or real centers. In addition, some proper measurement methods for these cyberspatial distance decays have to be developed.

4.3.2 *Distance Decay and Surfing to Specific Websites*

For Cairncross (1997), in her famous *Death of Distance* book and thesis, there should not have existed any distance decay patterns for the cost of transmission of electronic communications and information, given the high speed of digital information transmissions (see also Wang et al. 2003, p. 382). However, the emergence and evolution of Internet traffic has shown that information transmission operates otherwise, so that distance decay patterns have been identified for the virtual Internet, regarding the speeds of information transmissions for users' surfing to specific websites.

Some four years following the introduction of the universal and commercial Internet back in 1994, Murnion and Healy (1998) measured the duration, or the time that was needed, for movement in space or over distance, for electronic Internet signals traveling between users and the hosting servers for the websites with which they interacted. These durations were measured through pings and were coined as latency. Murnion and Healy (1998) were able to demonstrate that despite of the tiny transmission time differences, measured in milliseconds, distance-based gravity models for the number of website visitors could be drawn around the location of website hosting servers, thus presenting distance decay patterns for traffic around websites. In other words, the greater the physical distance between a user and a hosting server for a called website, the longer the two-way travel time for information transmitted between the user and the server. Five years later, in 2003, Wang et al. found, for US university networks, that distance still had an impact on Internet communications, but this impact was effective only for the first 1000 km of domestic distances between Internet users and contacted websites, and the equivalent first 3500 km for international distances among universities.

Later developments of Internet transmission technologies, mainly the invention and introduction of routers, peering and Internet hotels, side by side with infrastructure investments made for their wide adoption, have turned the very location of called websites more complex, thus permitting routing and destination flexibilities and alternations for the traffic between websites and their users. Eventually these developments have brought about further minimizations of latency differences, and avoiding, in most cases, the emergence of gravity models around website locations (Avidan and Kellerman 2004). Thus, the ping latency and its Gaussian spreading of inequality were shown to have been improved between 1998–2004 (Baker 2005). However, still in 2014, Obren and Howell (2014) demonstrated that the Internet 'tyranny of distance' in latency was still there for long-distance international data transmissions made to and from firms located in small and remote national economies, such as New Zealand. This latency existed despite heavy investments in transmission technologies, including broadband.

The study by Murnion and Healy (1998) of measured distance decays and gravity models for individual websites, or the supply side of the system, assumed implicitly that the server of each website constitutes a center, so that website users were scattered globally along distance from it, as measured by latency. By this type of distance decay, the Internet consists of millions of kind of 'local' centers, namely the hosting servers for websites. Back in mid-2014, the number of websites was estimated at close to one billion, with one quarter of these websites being active ones, thus presenting a tremendous growth since the universal introduction of the Internet in the mid-1990s (Internet live stats 2015). For websites hosted in Internet farms or hotels, several websites might be hosted in powerful hosting servers, but still peering or additional temporary locations for websites, in a rather global distribution, is possible.

4.3.3 Centrality and Navigation on the Internet

As we mentioned already, the second type of distance decay for the Internet, which we would like to propose here, is focused on the Internet end-users and their search activities, rather than on traffic to and around websites accessed specifically by users. In this type of distance decay for the Internet, discussed in the following paragraphs, the Internet screen space constitutes space (Kellerman 2016; Chap. 2), and the order of the search results presented on it presents distance decay from the first result item appearing on top of the screen downwards along the screen.

The search for information through search engines may sometimes involve an intensive experience of 'distance friction' by Internet users, as far as the required number of clicks they have to make, until they reach of a proper website, is concerned. This is so mainly when Internet users seek information on a specific topic without having any relevant websites in mind, as compared to surfing to specific websites, which we discussed before as pattern one for Internet distance decay. Such wider searches for information may involve extensive uses of search engines, as well as the related consulting of numerous websites. This effort implies not only an overcoming of distance, as measured by the number of clicks, but it involves also a kind of impedance, as measured by the time that is required for such search sessions. This digital impedance may be perceived as being similar to the one experienced in the driving of cars in real space, mainly for commuting (see e.g., Novaco et al. 1990). Thus, information search may involve the overcoming of cyberspatial distance, indicative through the time, convenience and level of complexity that typify surfing sessions for information search.

Internet users make use of either desktop or mobile communications devices, such as smartphones and tablets, as their use and access stations. Their search and surfing activities represent the demand side for information, whereas websites represent the supply side of the digital information base, the Web. Users are mostly insensitive to the micro time differences among electronic information flows, or latency, standing for distance measures of information flows. However, users are interested in the minimization of the time they have to spend for information searches, when looking for websites that will satisfy their needs for some specific information. As we noted, this search time may be viewed as distance friction, and sometimes even as an impediment. Similarly to the driving of cars in real space to specific street addresses while obeying general driving rules, each website has its own particular and non-hierarchical URL address, but all websites share identical rules and procedures for their access by Internet users.

Considering the notion of centrality from the perspective of Internet users, or the demand side of the Internet, sounds, at first glance, as complex, given the large numbers of both Internet users (or demand) and websites (or supply). We mentioned before the enormous supply sources for Internet information, standing in 2014 at some 250 million active websites (Internet live stats 2015). The demand side for Internet information is even larger, expressed by a huge and still growing number of Internet users worldwide, reaching some 3.2 billion individuals in 2015 (ITU 2015). These worldwide Internet users generated in 2015 over 100 billion monthly website searches, excluding direct surfing and accesses of specific websites (SEJ 2015). Under such high volumes of information sources, information seekers and information searches, where could the center of the virtual Internet be located in cyberspace? This question seems even more complicated if we take into account that the Internet is accessed and searched for endless purposes by its users. There are those users whose major interest is professional, looking for some most specific pieces of information, whereas others might prefer entertainment websites. For many additional users, both classes of websites might be relevant, but at different times of the day and the week.

One way of looking at centrality in the Internet is through the identification of the most popular websites worldwide, or the 'top sites', that were accessed by users worldwide. By the end of 2015, the top ten websites were by decreasing order of popularity: Google, Facebook, Youtube, Baidu (the leading Chinese search engine), Yahoo, Amazon, Wikipedia, Oq (China's most used Internet service portal), Google.co.in (the Indian version of Google), and Twitter (Alexa 2016). Of these leading websites, four are search engines, two are information sources, two are social networks, one is a portal, and just an additional one is a store.

As the list of leading, or most central, websites shows, the search for information/websites constitutes a leading need and, hence, also a leading Internet activity, satisfied by one special Internet tool, which serves all users for their information search activities, namely the search engines. For most users, search engines may constitute either their home page or they may appear as a bar on their homepage screens, as is true for both desktop computers and mobile ones, including smartphones. Search engines are in charge of the constant creation of Internet user-defined centers, as will be detailed below. Search engines may seem as a kind of a 'fixed' tool on most PCs, laptops, tablets, and smartphones, but their displayed contents, or the specific centers which they present, depend on the searched keywords, and these keywords change, of course, from search to search, as well as among users.

It has been reported that some 93 % of the Internet experiences of individual users begin with the use of search engines (SEJ 2015)! Numerous portals and websites include internal search engines for searches within them, and many of these search engines facilitate searches within additional related and linked websites as well, rather than in the whole Internet system. Other search engines are, of course, language and country specific ones. Our interest here will rather focus on system-wide, mainly English-language, search engines. There are only less than ten such general search engines that are used worldwide for system-wide searches, led by Google, Yahoo, Bing, and Ask. Of these, leadership has been held by Google for several years, with some 68.5 % of desktop searches made through it in May 2015 (Netmarketshare 2015).

It is, thus, possible to view general-purpose search engines as navigation tools, with the keywords inserted by users for the search of some information, as functioning like direction pointers. Search engines as navigation tools and keywords as direction pointers eventually lead to the most relevant website, or the center for any specific search, the address and description of which appearing on the top of the first page of search results. This desired result is followed by website descriptions and addresses for other websites of seemingly decreasing relevance, thus presenting distance decays from the center, namely the first result on the top of the first page of results proposed by the search engine. Such distance decays can be measured by the percentages of user selections of websites presented below the first result for their surfing to them. The centers of the Internet change, therefore, constantly and on an individual basis, from one search to another, so that for each search session a different center, or first result, is displayed. Thus, the number of Internet centers from the perspective of Internet users is truly immense and, of course, search specific.

The search engine industry constitutes a commercial business that functions as a leading force in the manipulation of Internet screens, in their capacity as virtual production landscapes, with varying locational costs charged for the location of results on users' result screens for website searches. These varying costs are based on the assumption that varying incomes may be derived by commercial entities which pay for preferred locations of their websites on Internet screens. The higher on the screen a website is presented the more frequent accesses to it are expected by the searching users.

4.3.4 *Structuring of Search Engine Distance Decay*

The structure and ordering of search engine results pages (SERPs), notably the first one, for searches of information involving any commercial meaning, reflect some most sophisticated marketing efforts, known as search engine marketing (SEM) (see e.g., Moran and Hunt 2014). Whereas searches for non-commercial information may yield the so-called organic search results, presenting first the results with the most fitting websites for the searched keywords, or the actual search query, the result pages for any search with a commercial connotation, notably the first one, are most carefully structured and ordered. We will demonstrate this through the first page of the Google search engine.

The first page of Google search results is normally divided into three sectors. On the left side of the screen, there might appear search-related paid ads, being marked as such, whereas on the right side there will appear website names or titles reflecting the searched keywords. The upper group of the results on the right side may normally present paid-for website names, addresses, and description, and they are usually marked as such. Under these paid-for website names, addresses, and descriptions, there appear results of listed websites, which are ordered by a declining fee paid for their appearance in specific ranks from the top of the list downwards. Google markets the paid-for ads and the prioritized ordering of the results under its 'AdWords' program, for monthly or for pay-for-click fees. These marketing tools provide the company with income, which permits the free use of its most extensive search engine (see e.g., Goodman 2008).

The first page, and sometimes also the following one, present, therefore, a highly complex virtual production landscape. The hidden assumption for the structure and ordering of these first pages is a decline in the attention to and use of the results by the searchers, or the click through rates (CTRs). This decline increases rapidly with growing distance from the top to the bottom of the page. In addition, the short texts for website contents, as appearing on the search result screens, may present attempts by website owners to satisfy searches made through as many keywords as possible, thus bringing about the appearance of their websites on the first page and in prioritized locations. These marketing efforts are known as search engine optimization (SEO).

Numerous professional studies in recent years have presented the average traffic share, or the click through rates (CTRs), for several search engines, notably for the leading Google (see e.g., Dearringer 2011; Petrescu 2014; Chitika Insights 2013). A similar line of study has emerged also in the academic literature, for touristic websites (Pan 2015), as well as for a variety of other searches analyzed through econometric modelling (Glick et al. 2014). These studies normally refer to the traffic share of the organic result positioning on the first results page, and to the traffic shares of the following result pages. All of these studies show exponential distance decay trends from the top result on the first page downwards. In the following paragraphs, as well as in Tables 4.1, 4.2 and Fig. 4.1, we will present the results of the Chitika Insights (2013) study.

The Chitika Insights study was based on 300 million US and Canadian page views made by some 100,000 Internet users who accessed more than 300,000 websites. The 2013 study findings were reported as being similar to the findings reported previously in a 2011 study, thus presenting some consistent trend. The 2013 study found that close to 92 % of the searchers consulted only the results that appeared on the first page of the Google results pages, or, in other words, the first page of the search results produced this percentage of Google traffic. This percentage declined dramatically for the following pages, with 4.8, 1.1, and 0.4 % for the second, third and fourth pages, respectively (Table 4.2). Clicks on the 15 organic results of the first page declined also exponentially, though a little less dramatically (Table 4.1 and Fig. 4.1). Thus, the top result on the first page yielded some 32.5 % of the total average traffic, followed by 17.6, 11.4 and 8.1 % for the second to fourth positions, respectively.

Table 4.1 Average traffic shares for Google first result page ranks, May 2013

Google first result-page rank	Average traffic share, or click through rates (CTRs), in percent
1	32.5
2	17.6
3	11.4
4	8.1
5	6.1
6	4.4
7	3.5
8	3.1
9	2.6
10	2.4
11	1
12	0.8
13	0.7
14	0.6
15	0.4

Source Chitika Insights (2013) the value of Google result positioning. https://chitika.com/google-positioning-value (with permission)

Table 4.2 Average traffic shares for Google result pages, May 2013

Google result page number	Average traffic share, or click through rates (CTRs), in percent
1	91.5
2	4.8
3	1.1
4	0.4
5	0.2
6	0.2
7	0.1
8	0.1
9	0.1
10	0.1

Source Chitika Insights (2013) the value of Google result positioning. https://chitika.com/google-positioning-value (with permission)

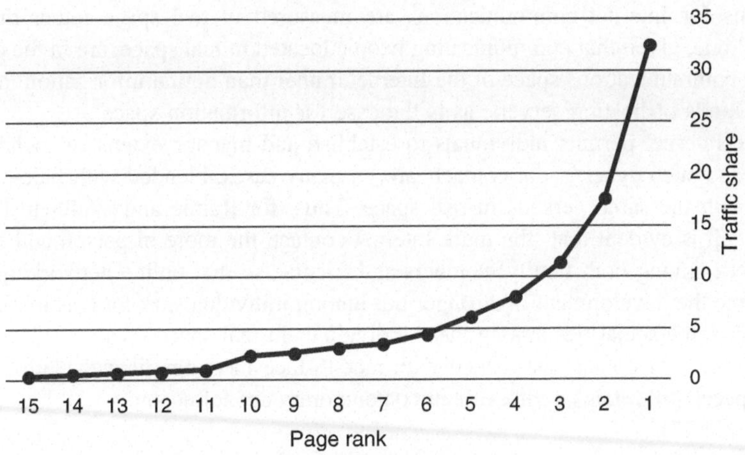

Fig. 4.1 Average traffic shares for Google first result page ranks, May 2013. *Data source* Chitika (2013) the value of Google result positioning. https://chitika.com/google-positioning-value (with permission)

There may emerge two patterns of distance decay for search sessions, functioning simultaneously and interactively, though they present opposite patterns of distance decay. If the search engine, or the navigation tool, is sophisticated enough and the keywords precisely phrased by the searching user, then the first result might serve as the center for a search session, with all other results presenting a distance decay pattern regarding the actual clicking or using of the proposed websites. However, if the search is not well defined by keywords, or if the search engine encounters some search difficulties, then users need to 'travel' outwards, or from the periphery (that is the first and dissatisfying result) to the center (lower located but satisfying results). Thus, the first result may serve in most searches as a center, but sometimes it may constitute a kind of periphery.

4.3.5 Distance Decay in Personal and Social Networking

The Web, or the information class of the Internet, which we have discussed so far, consists of information organized in websites, with Internet users either surfing directly to some specific websites, or searching, first, through search engines, in order to identify and reach proper websites. We presented in the previous subsections the existence of distance decay in both of these informational activities. The second class of the Internet, the communications space, consists mainly of e-mailing and Web 2.0 social networking platforms, which constitute channels for interpersonal communications. We will see in the following paragraphs that these activities also involve some distance decay patterns. However, these distance decay patterns for Internet communications are measured in real space rather than in virtual one, given that communicating people located in real space, are in the center of the communications space of the Internet, rather than digital information located in all kinds of hosting servers, as is the case for information space.

The Internet permits individuals to establish and manage extensive social contacts, and such cyberspatial contacts are, in many cases, blended with face-to-face ones with the same persons in real space. Thus, for Rainie and Wellman (2012, p. 127) it is evident that 'the more Internet contact, the more in person and phone contact', among both family members and friends, so that online networking may facilitate the development of stronger ties among individuals, as long as there exist already some social ties among these individuals in real space (Warf 2013). Given the richness of contact associated with face-to-face meetings, it was claimed that real space 'still retains a vital role in contemporary economic and social life' (Warf 2013, p. 147).

Social networking, in the form of interpersonal communications, nested within early e-mail and the Gopher cyberspatial communications systems, operating already before the introduction of the Internet as a wide and open access system in the mid-1990s, and eventually bringing about the emergence of global networks. Early networks developed initially around a physical location, e.g., the San Francisco-based WELL (Whole Earth 'Lectronic Link) network (see Rheingold 1993), whereas others, such as MOOs (MUD [Multi User Dungeon], Object Oriented), were organized around metaphorical cities, creating centrality and agglomeration within them through specific 'rooms', 'buildings', or 'neighborhoods', by topics of discussions and communications (see e.g., Schrag 1994).

A second generation of social networking, becoming popular as of the mid-1990s, consisted of on-line exchanges, via channels such as ICQ (I Seek You) and MSN (Microsoft Network), followed by blogs which were instituted as of 2002 (Herring et al. 2005), but were basically initiated in different forms much earlier

(Gopal 2007). Blogs and the 'blogsphere' constituted also part of the initial Internet platforms for global self-publications of personal materials by individuals.

The social networking dimension of the Internet has become extremely popular in the third phase of social networking through the emergence of the so-called Web 2.0, as of the mid-2000s, which aimed at the facilitation of interactive communications among networked subscribers. Web 2.0 has hosted since then several swiftly adopted networks or platforms for online social networking, led mainly by Facebook and Twitter, as well as by some additional well-known networks, such as MySpace, Linkedin, and Second Life.

Virtual social networking may include interactions taking place at varying geographical distances. For example, a popular use of Facebook is in its service as a framework for virtual interaction among school kids whose location may not stretch beyond a single neighborhood. Similarly, Facebook may facilitate online social relations among geographically close adult friends. These latter virtual ties are still the leading ones among all potential geographical extents of social networks, thus turning online networks into the new neighborhood (Rainie and Wellman 2012, pp. 13, 130–131; Kellerman 2014).

Mok et al. (2010) were able to show, in their longitudinal study of Toronto, that distance was still significant for human social relations, just before the massive adoption of online social networking. Comparing communications performances in Toronto through the period 1978 to 2005, they found that distance was still significant for communications along this whole period. The introduction of e-mail in the 1990s has brought about an increase in communications activity at large, with e-mailing preferred over face-to-face and telephone contacts. However, though e-mailing by its very nature is insensitive to distance, and thus may potentially lead to long distance communications, Mok et al. (2010) were able to demonstrate that the significance of distance for face-to-face and telephone contacts has remained unchanged between 1978 and 2005. Possibly, this trend may have continued even following the fast adoption of social networking platforms as of the mid-2000s. Thus, as mentioned already, Rainie and Wellman (2012, pp. 13, 130–131) believe that online social relations with geographically close friends are still the leading ones, turning online networks into the new neighborhood.

There is still a possibility, of which Turkle (2011, p. 154) warned, that individuals who may choose to remove themselves from physical social life because of online networked relations, may 'become less willing to get out there and take a chance'. On the other hand, however, one may ask 'are we engaged in the production of new spaces and new social relations, or merely simulating social structures in a hyperreal form? How does our experience of the global and the local, the public and the private, alter in a network society?' (Nunes 2006, p. xxiii).

Empirical studies of locational patterns for interpersonal and social contacts through the Internet, using e-mail and/or social networking, have been still scarce so far. However, the evidence presented above shows that there exists a distance decay in these contacts, as measured by the location of communicated people in real space. Generally then, the longer the physical distance separating the locations of Internet users and their contacts in real space, the less contacts would emerge among them in both real and virtual space, thus presenting distance decay patterns.

4.4 Distanciation

The geographical patterns for the extent of Internet uses present rather mixed trends. As we just stated, Internet communications and networking facilitate the potential emergence of contacts among Internet users without regard to distance. Still, however, users, as centers reaching out for some information and communications destinations, keep more Internet ties with physically closer people. Internet users may develop, though, potentially and frequently also practically, social and professional ties that are spread globally. In the information sphere of the Internet, Web surfers, in many cases, might not even be aware of the geographical location of the hosting servers for the websites that they consult. Still, there are users who may consult only websites of a rather domestic nature, and if only for linguistic preferences, whereas others may present a global distribution of the websites which they make use of.

Distanciation refers to the increasing geographical spread of potential destinations for human actions at large. For the use of the Internet, distanciation can be measured through the spatial extent of consulted websites by users, and the location of their contacted professional colleagues and social friends. The destinations for these informational and interpersonal activities can be domestic only, or they can be foreign ones as well, potentially reaching full globalization for the spread of Internet informational and/or interpersonal resources.

The increasing geographical spread of potential destinations for human actions, or the 'stretching' of the spread of social systems in time and space, was termed by Giddens (1990), at the time, as *distanciation*. This term originally referred to societal trends and processes, relating to societal abilities to reach further out in space and time since ancient times. Held (1995, p. 20; see also Amin 2002) referred to such 'stretching' specifically for contemporary society.

As we suggested in the opening paragraph for this section, the notion of distanciation may be extended also for the study of individual daily spatial actions. Contemporary virtual mobility technologies bring about a potential 'stretching' of individual spatial reach to its spatial global utmost, facilitated through their access of websites located anywhere. This global distanciation by Internet users may further be expressed in their possible involvement in remotely located affairs (see Adams 1998, p. 95).

The clicking efforts involved in reaching local, domestic or international websites, or for the contacting of people located at any distance, are the same (if the Internet addresses of desired websites and people are known). Individual distanciations assume free cyberspatial mobilities available to Internet users, something that may not be the case, though, under Internet censorships (see Warf 2013). If

Internet censorships, whether cultural or political, do not apply to all Internet users within a given national society, then this differentiation may reflect social classes, as we noted already with regard to boundaries (Sect. 3.4). For some users, the globally 'stretched' distanciation, which facilitates individual time and space free communications, has brought about the emergence of equally 'stretched', nationwide, and possibly also global and cross-border, communities, the so-called 'metageographic communities' (MGCs) (Nashleanas 2011).

The spatial extent of distanciation as presented by Internet users can be examined along the following lines, given our discussion so far. There might be users who would prefer to consult only domestic websites and interact only with people located close by in real space, whereas others may prefer to make use of websites and interact with other people located in specific other countries only. Some additional users may present a global extent of their distanciation, as expressed in the location and identity of the websites that they consult, as well as by the social and professional ties that they prefer to maintain.

4.5 Proximity

Proximity was defined as 'nearness in space, time, or relationship' (OED 2015b). Nearness or proximity among communicating people may develop in a stratified manner along numerous levels, through the availability of the wide variety of virtual communications platforms, including written, audial and visual media. Such a stratification of communications may fit, for example, evolving romantic or business relationships, the development of which may be expressed along the whole or part of the communications ladder, using changing virtual communications media, which would fit the changing phases of the relationship. Hence, only if two communicating parties feel comfortable enough, following their exchanges through virtual communications, then face-to-face contacting may be called for (Kellerman 2012).

At the earliest and lowest level of relationships, people may engage in lagged written exchanges, such as e-mails messages, and later on, they may move from these exchanges to online chats. These chats, on their part, may lead to real-time vocal conversations, which may be followed by video ones. Potentially then, these kinds of exchanges may serve as preparatory ones, eventually bringing about face-to-face meetings. Boden and Molotch (1994) assessed face-to-face meetings as having a crucial significance for interpersonal business contacts, in what they termed as the *compulsion of proximity*, and this conception was extended by Urry (2002) also for social contacts. In more routine communications, the choice of communications means per exchange may depend on the level of urgency for communications, and on the nature of the interaction.

We noted in our discussion of distanciation the potentially growing spatial expansion in users' reach of websites for their access and use of information, as well as the expansion of their social and professional ties. The distanciation of social contacts may be interconnected with stratified proximity. Particularly in spatially expanding interpersonal communications, the very availability of numerous written and oral communications channels may facilitate a desired level of proximity between communicating parties separated by long distances in real space. Such parties can make, therefore, use of e-mail and instant messaging tools, notably for their routine communications.

Additional communications media are still being developed. Of specific interest is the continued technological development of haptic devices, originally developed for video games. These devices permit virtual touching between people, and their possible introduction and adoption may bring about some change in the leveling and stratification of interpersonal communications, notably regarding proximity (Paterson 2006).

4.6 Conclusion

In this chapter we examined the status and significance of distance and its derivatives of distance decay, distanciation, and proximity, for the Internet per se, i.e. mainly within cyberspace itself. Distance, as a measure of separation, may be applied to the cyberspatial Internet by the number of clicks required either for the reaching of a desired specific piece of information or website, or for the reaching of specific people, in order to communicate with them.

Distance decay has been traditionally recognized as a basic pattern for spatial organization in real space. We presented distance decay patterns also for the two Internet classes of information and communications. There are two patterns of distance decay for the Internet information class. In surfing to specific websites, access duration to the websites increases with growing physical distance between hosting servers, which constitute centers, and users located around them by increasing physical distance/access time, as measured by latency through pings. In website searches via search engines, the order of search results, presented on Internet screens, is of special significance, since users prefer to access the first result, which serves, therefore, as a center on the Internet screen, with declining access by users to lower ranked results. In the Internet communications class, communications and networking permit contacts among Internet users without regard to distance. Still, users, as centers, keep more ties with physically closer people.

Generally, then, distance decay in the Internet presents diversified appearances, with hosting servers (for surfing), screen locations (for searching), and users' physical locations (for networking) as centers, and with varying decay measurements, respectively: time (for surfing), presentation ranking on screens (for searching), and physical distance (for contacting), respectively.

The most basic geographical notion of distance, which may seem, at a first glance, as difficult for a possible extension to the study of Internet information and communications spaces, turns out to be of crucial commercial importance in the ordering and structuring of search result screens. As in real space, distance decay may emerge only if there is a centered location around which it may develop, so that distance decay from centers is accompanied also by the existence of some kind of peripheries.

Distanciation refers to the increasing geographical spread of potential destinations for human actions at large. It can be measured also for the Internet through the spatial extent of consulted websites by users, as well as through the location in real space of their contacted professional colleagues and social friends. The destinations for these informational and interpersonal activities can be domestic only, or they can be foreign ones as well, potentially reaching globalization for the spread of Internet sources accessed by specific users.

Proximity, or nearness, among communicating people, may develop in a rather stratified manner along the numerous Internet communications media, facilitating written, audial and video communications. Such a stratification of communications may fit, for example, evolving romantic or business relationships, which may go up along the whole or part of the communications ladder from written, through audio to video communications, so that only if virtual communications prove satisfactory, then face-to-face contacting may be called for.

In summary, then, distance is relevant for the rather virtual cyberspace in several ways and for several of its components, varying along the several specific distance concepts. Distance in the Internet in general, and more so for the moving among websites, can be measured by the number of clicks needed for moving to desired websites or persons.

Cyberspatial distance involves also patterns of distance decay, and this in three ways. First, in direct surfing to specific websites some latency is involved, growing with the distance of users from the hosting servers of the desired website. Second, for search sessions, distance decay patterns emerge on Internet screens that present the search results. Thus, attention and followed use of proposed results decline exponentially from the top of the first results page downwards. Third, for interpersonal communications, the geographical pattern for the intensity of virtual communications presents distance decays from the physical locations of calling persons.

Side by side with the possible preference for social ties with people located nearby in physical space, the surfing and calling patterns of Internet users present trends of distanciation, or the 'stretching' of their spatial virtual reach, potentially reaching globalization. Internet communications facilitate stratified proximities between newly contacting parties, ranging from offline communications through online ones, to audial and video calls, and eventually to face-to-face ones. Levels of desired proximity may also determine the choice of communications means in routine contacting.

References

Adams, P. (1998). Network topologies and virtual place. *Annals of the Association of American Geographers, 88*, 88–106.

Alexa. (2016). Top sites. http://www.alexa.com/topsites.

Alonso, W. (1964). *Location and land use: Toward a general theory of land rent*. Cambridge, MA: Harvard University Press.

Amin, A. (2002). Spatialities of globalization. *Environment and Planning A, 34*, 385–399.

Ash, J. (2009). Emerging spatialities of the screen: Video games and the reconfiguration of spatial awareness. *Environment and Planning A, 41*, 2105–2124.

Avidan, I., & Kellerman, A. (2004). Distance in the Internet by time and route: An empirical examination. *Contemporary Israeli Geography: Horizons, 60–61*, 77–88.

Baker, R. G. V. (2005). Instantaneous global spatial interaction? Exploring the Gaussian inequality, distance and internet pings in global networks. *Journal of Geographical Systems, 7*, 361–379.

Boden, D., & Molotch, H. L. (1994). The compulsion of proximity. In R. Friedland & D. Boden (Eds.), *NowHere Space, Time and Modernity* (pp. 257–286). Berekeley: University of California Press.

Cairncross, F. (1997). *The death of distance: How the communications revolution will change our lives*. Boston: Harvard Business School Press.

Chitika Insights. (2013). The value of Google result positioning (https://chitika.com/google-positioning-value).

Couclelis, H. (1996). Editorial: The death of distance. *Environment and Planning B: Planning and Design, 23*, 387–389.

Dearringer, J. (2011). A tale of two studies: Google vs. Bing click-through- rate. Moz Blog (https://moz.com/blog/a-tale-of-two-studies-google-vs-bing-clickthrough-rate).

Giddens, A. (1990). *The Consequences of Modernity*. Cambridge: Polity Press.

Glick, M., Richards, G., Sapozhnikov, M., & Seabright, P. (2014). How does ranking affect user choice in online search? *Review of Industrial Organization, 45*, 99–119.

Goodman, E. (2008). *Winning results with google AdWords* (2nd ed.). New York: McGraw Hill.

Gopal, S. (2007). The evolving social geography of blogs. In H. J. Miller (Ed.), *Societies and Cities in the age of instant access* (pp. 275–293). Dordrecht: Springer.

Held, D. (1995). *Democracy and the global order*. Cambridge: Polity Press.

Herring, S. C., Scheidt, L. A., Wright, E., & Bonus, S. (2005). Weblogs as bridging genre. *Information Technology and People, 18*, 142–171.

Internet live stats. (2015). Total number of Webites. http://www.internetlivestats.com/total-number-of-websites/).

ITU (International Telecommunication Union). (2015). ICT Facts and Figures: The World in 2015 (http://www.itu.int/en/ITU-D/Statistics/Documents/facts/ICTFactsFigures2015.pdf).

Kellerman, A. (1983). Economic and spatial aspects of von Thunen's factor intensity theory. *Environment and Planning A, 15*, 1521–1530.

Kellerman, A. (1989a). Agricultural location theory 1: Basic models. *Environment and Planning A, 21*, 1381–1396.

Kellerman, A. (1989b). Agricultural location theory 2: Relaxation of assumptions and applications. *Environment and Planning A, 21*, 1427–1446.

Kellerman, A. (2012). *Daily spatial mobilities: Physical and virtual*. Farnham and Burlington, VT: Ashgate.

Kellerman, A. (2014). *The internet as second action space*. London and New York: Routledge.

Kellerman, A. (2016). Image spaces and the geography of internet screen-space. *GeoJournal, 81* (forthcoming), doi:10.1007/s10708-015-9639-1.

Kwan, M.-P. (2001). Cyberspatial cognition and individual access to information: The behavioral foundation of cybergeography. *Environment and Planning B, 28*, 21–37.

Mok, D., Wellman, B., & Carrasco, J. (2010). Does distance matter in the age of the internet? *Urban Studies, 47*, 2747–2783.

Moran, M., & Hunt, B. (2014). *Search Engine Management Inc: Driving search traffic to your company's website* (3rd ed.). Indianapolis, IN: IBM Press.

Murnion, S., & Healey, R. G. (1998). Modeling distance decay effects in Web server information flows. *Geographical Analysis, 30*, 285–303.

Nashleanas, K. (2011). Metageographic communities: A geographic model of demassified societies. *Annals of the Association of American Geographers, 101*, 625–649.

Netmarketshare. (2015). Desktop search engine market share https://www.netmarketshare.com/search-engine-market-share.aspx?qprid=4&qpcusto.

Novaco, R., Stokols, W., & Milanesi, L. (1990). Objective and subjective dimensions of travel impedance as determinants of commuting stress. *American Journal of Community Psychology, 18*, 231–257.

Nunes, M. (2006). *Cyberspaces of everyday life*. Minneapolis: University of Minnesota Press.

Obren, M., & Howell, B. (2014). The tyranny of distance prevails: HTTP protocol latency and returns to fast fibre internet access network deployment in remote economies. *Annals of Regional Science, 52*, 65–85.

OED (Oxford English Dictionaries). (2015a). Distance. http://www.oxforddictionaries.com/definition/english/distance.

OED (Oxford English Dictionaries). (2015b). Proximity. http://www.oxforddictionaries.com/definition/english/proximity.

Pan, B. (2015). The power of search engine ranking for tourist destinations. *Tourism Management, 47*, 79–87.

Paterson, M. (2006). Feel the presence: Technologies of touch and distance. *Environment and Planning D: Society and Space, 24*, 691–708.

Petrescu, P. (2014). Google organic click-through rates in 2014. Moz Blog https://moz.com/blog/google-organic-click-through-rates-in-2014.

Pons-Novell, J., & Viladecans-Marsal, E. (2006). Cities and the internet: The end of distance? *Journal of Urban Technology, 13*, 109–131.

Rainie, L., & Wellman, B. (2012). *Networked: The new social operating system*. Cambridge, MA: MIT Press.

Rheingold, H. (1993). A slice of life in my virtual community. In L. M. Harasim (Ed.), *Global networks: Computers and international communication* (pp. 57–82). Cambridge, MA: MIT Press.

Schrag, Z. M. (1994). Navigating cyberspace—maps and agents: Different uses of computer networks call for different interfaces. In G. C. Staple (Ed.), *Telegeography 1994: Global telecommunications traffic* (pp. 44–52). Washington, DC: Telegeography Inc.

SEJ (Search Engine Journal). (2015). 24 eye-popping SEO statistics. http://www.searchenginejournal.com/24-eye-popping-seo-statistics/42665/.

Sui, Z. S. (2004). Tobler's first law of geography: A big idea for a small world? *Annals of the Association of American Geographers, 94*, 269–277.

Tobler, W. (1970). A computer movie simulating urban growth in the Detroit region. *Economic Geography, 46*, 234–240.

Turkle, S. (2011). *Alone together: Why we expect more from technology and less from each other*. New York: BASIC BOOKS.

Urry, J. (2002). Mobility and proximity. *Sociology, 36*, 255–274.

Wang, Y., Lai, P., & Sui, D. (2003). Mapping the Internet using GIS: The death of distance hypothesis revisited. *Journal of Geographical Systems, 5*, 381–405.

Warf, B. (2013). *Global geographies of the internet*. Dordrecht: Springer.

Weinberger, D. (2002). *Small pieces loosely joined {a unified theory of the web}*. Cambridge, MA: Perseus.

Yu, H., & Shaw, S.-L. (2008). Exploring potential human activities in physical and virtual spaces: A spatio-temporal GIS approach. *International Journal of Geographical Information Science, 22*, 409–430.

Chapter 5
Mobility Over the Internet

Abstract Mobilities in both physical and virtual spaces, have received growing attention by contemporary scholars. The notion of cyber-mobility will be reviewed first, followed by discussions of the following specific notions, as for their relevance for Internet analysis: flow, speed, directionality, circularity, co-presence, and time-space compression. Internet co-presence evolves for all the four elements sought by individuals in space at large: fellow people, places, times and information. All the four elements, and the co-presence which they involve, will be presented in detail. Meaningful co-presence is not something that is just there, developing or occurring automatically, but it requires some activation by relevant Internet users.

Keywords Cyber-mobility · Flow · Speed · Directionality · Circularity · Co-presence · Time-space compression

Our systematic geographical interpretation of the Internet moves now into its fourth phase. Starting with an elaboration of the Internet as space, we then attempted continued with an attempt to discover cyberspatial geographical structures, followed by discussions on separations (distance) within the Internet. It is now time for us to explore a fourth geographical dimension, that of mobility over the Internet. We will attempt to explore Internet mobility using some of the terminology that has been developed in this regard, mainly within geography and sociology, as part of the emerging field of mobility studies. Given our accent on individual uses of the Internet, the particular study of personal mobilities, for both physical and virtual spaces, is of special relevance (see e.g. Kellerman 2006a, 2012).

The discussions in this chapter will differ somehow from those in the two previous ones, in that the explorations in this chapter will focus on concepts that were proposed simultaneously for the study of personal mobilities in both real space and cyberspace. We will present in this chapter, first, the notion of cyber-mobility, referring to the very mobility of people through the Internet, followed by discussions of six specific mobility notions. We will delve into explorations as for the levels and ways of relevance of these terms for geographic interpretations of the

A. Kellerman, *Geographic Interpretations of the Internet*,
SpringerBriefs in Geography, DOI 10.1007/978-3-319-33804-0_5

Internet. These six notions are defined below specifically as terms for the geographical interpretation of the Internet:

Flow—the sequence of Internet screens, with each screen requiring some action by Internet users.
Speed—Internet data transmission and user interaction speeds.
Directionality—the possible existence of spatial destinations in Internet surfing.
Circularity—repetitive movements by Internet users between the same websites of origin and destination.
Co-presence—synchronous presence of Internet users in both real and virtual spaces in the performance of a variety of interpersonal communications over the Internet.
Time-space compression—compression of the dimensions of time and space through continuous Internet communications.

5.1 Cyber-Mobility

Cyber-mobility constitutes mobility through the cyberspatial Internet. Obviously, this cyber-mobility may only refer to the movements of information, in all of its types and forms, since people and goods (other than money) cannot yet move or be moved through the Internet system. However, the extremely wide abilities that are facilitated by the Internet for the speedy movements of information, side by side with the ability for Internet users to perform online textual, audial and visual communications, makes users feel as if they themselves are on the go, involved in some movement activity, or being mobile. Thus, cyber-mobility refers also to people in some way, and not just to information of any kind.

The Internet has expanded personal virtual mobility turning it into a democratic right, through its provision of instant written communications, as well as through its facilitation of individual access to information. It has practically extended personal virtual expression, in personal as well as in public forums, to unprecedented levels, through personal websites, social networking platforms, side by side with e-mail correspondence.

Cyber-mobility has become increasingly significant along the introduction and adoption of technological innovations for the use of the Internet. Thus, until the introduction of fixed broadband, cyberspace was accessible to Internet subscribers as an entity being completely separate from real space entities, since it required logging into the system, it involved payment per time use, and it offered slow functioning and limited functionality. Fixed broadband has changed all this, by permitting constant connection, fast responses and growing numbers of applications for daily uses. The following introduction and adoption of mobile broadband amounted to the availability of these amenities without fixed locations and without time constraints (Kellerman 2014). Hence, mobile broadband has turned the

Internet into a routine component of daily life, without any barriers of access, thus eliminating any preexisting conceptual separation between cyberspace and real space.

Cyber-mobility when using smartphones has been routinely integrated with several aspects of real space. It implies a blurring between the private and the public, as well as between indoors and outdoors (Kopomaa 2000), becoming into what Sheller (2004) termed 'mobile publics'. Specifically, Internet surfing while being on the move accentuates placelessness (Relph 1976; Chap. 3), or the lack of clear grounded anchoring for Internet users. On the other hand, however, under conditions of enhanced virtual mobilities for interpersonal communications, places may be viewed now as foci of social relations. Thus, 'if one moves in from the satellite to the globe, holding all those networks of social relations and movements and communications in one's head, then each 'place' can be seen as a particular, unique, point of their intersection' (Massey 2008, p. 262).

The use of mobile broadband may also carry implications for the meaning of urban physical space for both local residents and visitors of cities. The constant availability of GPS (Global Positioning System), while walking or driving through unknown urban spaces, implies an efficient moving of people through urban space, thus saving time and efforts in walking, driving, and searching. However, this moving about cities turns the crossed streets and urban space in general into a kind of impediment rather than into a cultural occasion for the exploration of urban space. Such loss of meaning of urban space may occur also when smartphone users located in urban space are continuously engaged in social networking and information searches.

5.2 Flow

The notion of 'flow', mainly within the mobility context, has normally been interpreted through rather macro connotations, referring to material, virtual or abstract movements within given systems. Thus, generally, the movement of information was compared to the movement of gas, characterized by utmost moving flexibility, as compared to the movement of people (which is similar in its level of flexibility to the movement of liquids), and that of commodities (which constitutes the movement of solid entitites) (Kellerman 1993, p. 160). Urry (2000, 2003a) used the metaphor of fluids as a general term for the things that are being moved globally, such as information, capital, risks, etc. In his discussion of fluids for mobility, he claimed that 'any such fluid can be distinguished in terms of the *rate* of flow, its *viscosity*, the *depth*, its *consistency*, and its degree of *confinement*' (Urry 2000, p. 32).

The Internet was considered to constitute 'a metaphor for the social life as fluid' (Urry 2000, p. 40). The flows of social life as fluid are channeled through networks with varying degrees of flexibility. Social networks are most flexible ones, with participants joining and leaving them freely, and with subscribers preferring to keep their anonymity in many cases. Other networks, such as commercial ones, owned by sellers of commodities and services, may consist of one-way flows, from the owners to their clientele, with identities of subscribers revealed and used by network managements, for the distribution, for instance, of promotional materials. Networks that are more rigid in their operations are, for example, Intranets, which are open only to employees of specific companies. Even more restricted in their access, and for obvious reasons, are banking or inter-bank networks, such as the global SWIFT (Society for Worldwide Interbank Financial Telecommunication), characterized by strictly controlled and monitored flows.

Flow can constitute also a rather individual experience when using the Internet. Such an experience may be similar to the experience of driving a car in a city. The specific structures of a road system, the driving alternatives that it facilitates, and its eventual specific uses, as conditioned by the levels of traffic congestion, may bring about varying experiences for drivers, as far as trip length and convenience are concerned. Similarly, flow in the Internet for individual users may refer to the sequence of screens that follow each other in the use of websites, notably those websites that provide some service, with each screen requiring some action by Internet users, for instance when engaged in financial transactions, shopping, travel reservations, etc. Users may encounter friendly and logical flows of processes/screens, or rather cumbersome or complicated ones, making it difficult for them to follow through. Flows for individuals in cyberspatial contexts refer, therefore, to the flows of information, as well as to the flows of the interactions of users with a website (or with the server behind it). Thus, flows can be measured in two ways: by the rate of unsuccessful completions of transactions per website, and/or by the time it takes for the completion of successful ones.

A growing number and variety of Internet operations performed by individuals, notably those that replace face-to-face operations in real space, characterize the contemporary Internet. Such operations frequently require the use of numerous screens for operations with forms, signatures, certifications, etc. (Kellerman 2014). This is typical for banking, shopping, reservations, and governmental procedures. The structuring of websites as customer friendly ones, in terms of the optimization and convenience of information flows along numerous screens, has become a major concern for owners of relevant websites, in order to encourage customers to perform their daily activities over the Internet, instead of in the more costly real space service facilities (see e.g. COPC 2016).

5.3 Speed

Speed, as a contemporary societal value, was viewed as 'an irresistible temptation beyond reasonable rational calculation' (Hägerstrand 1992, p. 35). As such, 'speed is the premier cultural icon of modern societies…Speed symbolizes manliness, progress, and dynamism' (Freund and Martin 1993, p. 89). Hence, long before the introduction of the commercial Internet, Virilio (1983, p. 5) called our era the 'age of the accelerator', and he further claimed that 'the military-industrial democracies have managed to transform all social categories into the unknown soldiers of the Order of Speed' (Virilio 1977, p. 120).

Speed has been expressed in the features of immediacy and instantaneity that have accompanied the innovation and adoption of devices for electronic telecommunications, as some of their leading qualities. Immediacy and instantaneity have been recently accentuated through the growing contemporary rush for the production and consumption of increasing fixed and mobile broadband Internet speeds in developed countries. This rush presents a desire by both developers and users to avoid any differentiation in immediacy and instantaneity between vocal connections, on the one hand, and the transmission of the heaviest files of data or of streaming pictures, on the other. Thus, transmission speeds have become a crucial element for the emergence of the Internet as an action space for the performance of a variety of daily activities (Kellerman 2014). Growing transmission speeds have also facilitated a growing personalization of entertainment habits, since Internet subscribers may download selected music pieces and full movies to their own computers and smartphones extremely fast, and then enjoy them instantly at any time and place. Broadband is less critical for Internet communications activities, other than video calls, in which broadband permits flowing video conversations.

The tremendous importance of speed as a leading social value in contemporary societies may have stemmed from the expansive nature of capitalism, and it may further serve its continued growth (see Freund and Martin 1993). Thus, higher speeds for the transmissions of information and resources in general, and of capital in particular, may potentially intensify economic activity. Specifically, higher transmission speeds may also enhance the management of facilities that are spread and dispersed widely in real space, thus bringing about increased profits (see Harvey 1989).

The use of high speeds by individual Internet users involves a cost. Whereas before the introduction of broadband communications the use of the Internet was priced through the duration of use sessions, currently the cost of Internet use, is priced by bandwidth, so that the wider it is the more expensive its cost. Wider bandwidth imply speedier Internet uses for all purposes. Thus, the digital gap between developed and developing countries, in which broadband is frequently not available, is now reflected not just in the very access to the Internet, but in its speed, as well. In developed countries, the differentiation in speed may reflect social classes and social inequality, and when many services are offered to citizens mainly through the Internet, a remarkably slower use of the system may turn out as a major constraint in the conduct of daily lives, thus potentially widening economic, social and educational gaps among social sectors and groups.

The rush for fixed broadband installations has been led by South Korea, in which already in early 2014 practically all Internet subscribers enjoyed broadband connection (ITU 2015). However, the highest average mobile broadband speed was available in 2015 rather in Spain with 18 Mbps (Megabytes per second), followed by Denmark, Finland and South Korea with an average mobile broadband speed of some 17 Mbps in each country (Time 2015). Spain is a newcomer to the list of leading countries in telecommunications infrastructures and services, attesting to the competitive environment among EU countries regarding broadband speed levels. South Korea, on the other hand, has led in the adoption of broadband since its introduction in the 1990s (Kellerman 2006b), whereas Scandinavian countries have led in the adoption of telecommunications innovations in general, since closely after the innovation of the telephone in the late nineteenth century (Kellerman 1999). The growing dependence of individuals on broadband connectivity for a wide variety of applications and daily matters, accentuates the inter-sectoral and international digital gaps that still exist, and these refer now not merely to the very access to the Internet, but also to its speed qualities and pricing (see Chap. 1).

The actual speed of transmission for specific Internet actions performed by individuals may vary among Internet subscribers, even when they operate under the same broadband speed programs, given the prevailing local transmission conditions at given times and places. Such differences in communication speeds among particular transmissions can be measured through the ping utility (Kwan 2001; Avidan and Kellerman 2004; Chap. 4).

By their very nature, the two notions of speed and flow for Internet operations, mainly in its information space of websites, are closely related to each other. Users would need both parameters operating at sufficient levels in order for them to perform satisfactorily their daily operations over the Internet.

5.4 Directionality

Directionality was denoted by sociologists as the existence of some predefined spatial destinations for specific movements (see Bonss and Kesselring 2004; Kesselring and Vogl 2004). In real space, most of our walking movements are directional, namely that they are geared towards predefined destinations. However, some pedestrians might perform non-directional walks, when the very walking and/or wandering are the trip objectives rather than the reaching of some specific destinations (see Goffman 1971, p. 28; De Certeau 1985, p. 129).

In car driving, trips are almost always directional, so that the routing of trips is geared towards the reaching of a planned destination. Since most of people's walking trips and almost all of their driving trips involve some predefined directionality or destinations, this parameter has normally not been measured in any particular way for these real space mobilities.

The distinction between users who choose either directional or non-directional destinations, which can be easily detected for physical travel, cannot be simply applied to Internet mobility, and the directionality patterns there may turn out more complex for the uses of both the Internet communications and information spaces.

In the Internet communications sphere, e-mail messages are directed to persons through their cyberspatial addresses, rather than to their physical addresses, so that addressees may retrieve their messages through computers or mobile phones located anywhere, and not necessarily at any predesignated computers with unique physical and rather fixed locations.

For uses of the Internet information space, when using the Web for the search of information on a certain topic, the directionality of the search process is pointed to the website of a specific search engine. However, this is actually only an interim directionality, whereas the directionality, or the destination, for the desired information is completely open, given the very nature of the search, which is looking for websites that would fit some specific information searches.

In surf sessions that are directed to specific websites, there is no clear-cut directionality that can be addressed to the locations of such specific websites in real space, since in many cases information may be transmitted to users from peering servers and not necessarily from the hosting server for that the accessed website. Furthermore, in most cases surfers are not necessarily interested in the location of hosting servers, but rather in the identity of the information providers and, of course, in the information itself.

Generally then, Internet users seek information without regard of the geographical transmission origin in real space of the desired information. Therefore, cyberspatial directionality refers to Internet destinations, namely people in the communications space, and websites or information, in the information space. The real space locations for these destinations seem irrelevant in most cases. However, users may still be interested in the identity of the organizations or companies that own specific websites, in order to check whether the information or transaction, which are offered by these websites, can be trusted. Thus, from time to time, users may examine the directionality of their Internet activities, in terms of the institutional sources of information, but not in terms of its rather flexible geographical sourcing via hosting servers. The location of the servers that hosted websites from which information was transmitted to users at specific surfing sessions, as well as the routing of the transmitted information, can be traced through programs such as Neotrace (2015) (see also Avidan and Kellerman 2004).

From yet another, and completely different, perspective of directionality, the Internet permits multidirectional movements within and between websites, namely forward, backward, as well as nonlinear movements (Kwan 2001). Obviously, the number and frequencies of such movements, as performed by individual users, can be counted, and, thus, measured.

Websites may further be assessed for directionality, if they facilitate communications of users with website owners, thus becoming two-way directed websites, or whether they do not provide for such communications, thus being only one-way directed websites, which facilitate the transmission of information from one-to-many, or from the website owners to their clientele, only.

5.5 Circularity

Circularity refers to repetitive, frequently also cyclical, movements between the same origins and destinations. In the physical world, the routine example for circularity is commuting (see Amin and Thrift 2002, pp. 81–83). Commuting is not only circular but it is also cyclical, since commuters have a daily mobility cycle on weekdays, leaving their homes for work and returning there at the end of their daily work cycle. Patterns of circularity and cyclicality of individual mobilities within their daily temporal and spatial contexts have been studied mainly using the time-space prism and the time geography framework, both of which were proposed at the time by Hägerstrand (1970, 1973, 1975).

Circular movements constitute the usual case for Internet users who return normally to their home page at the end of use sessions, but users may alternatively prefer to disconnect from the Web. In addition, frequently Internet surfers may reach more than just a single destination, so that they may surf to numerous websites in sequence before returning to their homepage. This circularity pattern is similar to the case for many, if not most, of commuting trips involving, for example, shopping trips made directly after work before reaching home. Some Internet use sessions may frequently be cyclical, for instance, when the same website is being used periodically, such as for scheduled checking of bank accounts. Both the circularity and cyclicality of Internet use sessions can be simply measured by noting the three basic parameters for a movement session: the specific websites from which a surfing session begins, the websites visited during the session, and the website in which the session concluded.

5.6 Co-presence

Co-presence constitutes a condition that signifies any use of, or presence in, cyberspace, while being simultaneously located in real space. In some way, therefore, co-presence is a form of co-location, but 'presence' seems to be a more appropriate term for being in cyberspace, rather than 'location', which carries a more material connotation. As Kwan (2001, p. 26) claimed regarding the cognitive significance of co-presence: 'the contradictory experience of being somewhere and nowhere at the same time is perhaps the most obvious cognitive dissonance resulting from the use of the WWW'. The massive adoption of smartphones has turned co-presence into routine and often into continuous experiences, thus bringing Arminen (2007) to note on the 'dual nature for mobile media, making them both global and local' (p. 432). Co-presence constitutes a basic geographical experience in the use of the Internet, and, as we will see, it is multi-dimensional in nature, accompanying the exposure of users to fellow users, as well as the users' contacting with places, events, information, and even with things. These wide-ranging occurrences of co-presence through the use of the Internet invite some detailed attention to it, as we will do in the following discussions.

The more general notion of *presence*, as well as its literature, have been widely discussed, listed, and reviewed elsewhere, albeit mostly not by geographers, despite its strong geographical connotation (see e.g. Emerson et al. 1999; IJsselsteijn et al. 2001; Lombard and Jones 2007). Regarding presence as related to virtual space it was suggested to merge the rather separate notions of telepresence, virtual presence and presence into unified and more general notions of presence, as an experience (Lee 2004), or as a feeling (Schubert 2009).

Our discussion here will rather focus on the relatively less-studied presence class and notion of *co-presence*, which requires some attention and a systematic elaboration in our mobility age, since the flourishing and the widely adopted mobile information technologies for personal use, extend the options and occasions for co-presence, both veteran and novel ones. We will attempt to elaborate on co-presence from a functional perspective, thus referring to its practical occurrence among individuals. We will further attempt to highlight several contemporary patterns for co-presence in developed countries, all under the assumption of the wide adoption and use of highly developed technologies for virtual personal mobility. In addition, we will attempt to explore some emerging combinations among several of the co-presence patterns, which we will highlight in the following discussions.

By their very nature, the following elaborations on co-presence will focus on users' co-presence experiences *vis-à-vis* the cyberspatial Internet, side by side with the highlighting of the co-presence medium, namely the Internet and its components that are relevant for these experiences. This focus here is, thus, different from the one in our previous discussions of geographical parameters and terms, and their possible application to cyberspace, which tended more to the highlighting of the medium, the Internet, rather than to focusing on its personal experiencing. Furthermore, co-presence is not a measureable condition, so that it is difficult to identify levels of co-presence. Co-presence is rather a matter of existence or non-existence.

5.6.1 Definitions for Co-presence

The Oxford reference (2015) has proposed several connotations and dimensions for co-presence (with their numbering added here):

1. Most broadly, any close occurrence of different things.
2. The simultaneous presence of individuals in the same location, not necessarily engaged in face-to-face interaction with each other.
3. The engagement of individuals in synchronous interpersonal communication, not necessarily in the same physical location (e.g. using mobile phones) (co-present interaction).
4. In any form of mediated communication, the phenomenological sense of 'being there' with another person in place and/or time.
5. In presence studies, how an individual's sense of 'being there' in a virtual environment is affected by the presence of others who are also inside the simulation in the form of avatars.

For Ling (2008), for instance, co-presence along the second dimension quoted above, which focuses on the simultaneous presence of individuals in the same location, would require some interaction among these co-present individuals. However, as Farman (2012) noted, co-presence may now be mediated electronically, as proposed by the third dimension of co-presence quoted above. This third dimension of virtual co-presence was differentially termed as ‘absent presence’ (Gergen 2002), ‘virtual proximity’ (Baumann 2003), and ‘digital elasticity’ (Pearce and Gretzel 2012) (see also Germann-Molz and Morris-Paris 2015).

The three latter dimensions for co-presence out of the five ones proposed above clearly assume and reflect the availability and use of contemporary communications technologies, thus providing for new forms of co-presence and their related sensing of ‘being there’. We will concentrate here mainly on the dimensions/definitions 2 and 3 as proposed above for co-presence, focusing on the very occurrence of co-presence in physical and mostly in virtual settings. Our discussion will employ numerous notions and observations that have been suggested so far for the study of co-presence in several disciplines, as well as on observations and notions that have been proposed for the study of adjacent topics.

The following discussions will begin with an exposition of the nature of co-presence, focusing on co-presences with fellow people, events, places, information and things. Following this exposition, some more detailed discussions of co-presences of people in physical and virtual spaces will be presented, and these will be continued by separate elaborations on co-presences with places and information sources. Following the highlighting of these co-presence patterns, we will move to the exploration of two more complex patterns of co-presence: simultaneous multiple co-presences, and co-presences in the city. Finally, we will conclude with a general discussion of contemporary co-presence modes.

5.6.2 *The Nature and Types of Co-presence*

People may find themselves engaged in some form of physical-virtual co-presence because they were drawn to get in touch by at least one out of five attractions. First, and most frequently, individuals might be eager or they might be in some need to meet and communicate with fellow people, either through face-to-face encounters or through any of the numerous currently available audial and/or visual communications media. Second, individuals may wish or they may need to visit places virtually (*obligations to place* á la Urry 2003b). Third, people may prefer to remotely attend events through virtual media (*event obligations* á la Urry 2003b). Remote event attendance is the only co-presence attraction that can so far take the form of *mass co-presence*, mostly through television, but now also through Internet direct broadcasting technologies, both options permitting millions of people to remotely attend events, usually sport competitions. Fourth, individuals may wish to consult or interact with any kind of Internet information resources, imported to their computers or smartphones (Kellerman 2012).

A fifth attraction for co-presence is now in its first steps of development and adoption, namely the co-presence of people with things, such as household appliances, through the emerging *Internet of things* (IoT), or the possible remote operation, monitoring and control of machinery and appliances through the Internet, including household devices, such as washing machines, stoves, and heating systems. This last and new line of co-presence through the Internet, may involve some, still unforeseen, regulatory and social changes, as well as some geographical ones, permitting, for instance, some more flexible home visits (see e.g. Skarauskiene and Kalinauskas 2015). From a geographical perspective, the Internet of things amounts to the operation and control of things in physical space by the Internet in cyberspace (see Kitchin and Dodge 2011).

It is, therefore, for fellow people, places, times, information, and things, to bring about some co-presence by their seekers, and in more general terms, reaching out by individuals in the mobility/information age, involves now several modes of co-presence. Moreover, with the use of mobile communications technologies, one might be located in full physical isolation from fellow humans, but still experience abundant, albeit virtual, co-presences with people, events, places and information.

All five stimuli for reaching out (people, places, events, information, and things) which involve co-presences, as well as the use of human and technological means for their materialization, require some initiation and activation by individuals, in order for any meaningful co-presence to emerge. With a few exceptions, such as the passive presence of numerous people next to each other in public, mostly urban, locations, meaningful co-presence is not something that is just there, developing or occurring automatically.

The spatial extent for activities of all five types that involve virtual co-presence constitutes an integral part of the actual activity space of individuals. This activity space may be identical to the rather potential action space of individuals, if they make use of mobile broadband communication, since broadband communications permits global access, and therefore facilitates global reaching out by individuals (see Kellerman 2014). Table 5.1 presents several aspects of the five co-presence attractions that can be reached virtually: preparatory coordination; involved senses; partners and called places. We will shortly outline and discuss these aspects below.

Co-presence in a virtual conversation, mainly a video one, may normally require some preparatory coordination, usually through another call, such as a chat or a message. However, audial calls may obviously take place even without prior

Table 5.1 Attractions for virtual co-presence and their aspects

Aspect ⟹ Attraction ⬇	Coordination	Senses	Partners	Called place
People	Normally required	At least hearing and speech	At least two	Mobile
Events	Required	Hearing and vision	At least two	Fixed
Places	Not required	At least vision	One	Fixed
Information	Not required	Vision for texts	One	Flexible
Things	Not required	Vision and hearing	One	Fixed

coordination, with a chance of delayed communications due to absence of the called partner. However, the remote online 'live' attendance of an event requires the scheduling of the event attendance by its attendees, given the specific timing of the event, which applies to all attendees. The meeting of places, by its very nature, does not require any coordination, which is also true for the use of information online, or for the contacting of things.

Co-presence requires the employing of basic human senses in varying complexities. Interestingly enough, the co-presence stimulus that developed relatively late in the evolution of the human race, textual information, becoming relevant only as of the emergence of written languages, requires the use of vision only. The use of contemporary digital information may require also the employing of hearing, either for music or for films. Event attendance, physical or virtual, requires the use of both vision and hearing, whereas encounters with places turn out to be more complex. Virtual co-presences with places may need the use of vision only, but physical visits to places may be fully experienced only if the four senses of vision, hearing, touching and smelling are used. Co-presence with people, probably being the most basic kind of co-presence, requires in its ultimate and mostly intimate occasions, the use of all five senses, including also speech. However, contemporarily available technologies for virtual co-presence with people exclude the ability to use smelling and touching. Finally, the upcoming introduction of co-presence with things, will require the use of vision and probably also of hearing for the reception of alerts.

Co-presence with people obviously requires a minimum of one partner, so that at least two parties are involved in any kind of interaction. This applies also for event attendance, in case the event consists of a presentation by one person only. However, for the meeting of, or co-presence with, places, information, and things, just one person, a specific Internet user, is normally involved.

The called place in an interaction between or among people might be mobile, if the called person is on the move, and this may apply also to the calling party, as well as to both partners. An event, though, normally takes place in a fixed location, which applies also to the watching of rather fixed places or landscapes. Still, however, the calling party for event presence or place watching might be on the move. The location of an information source, normally a website, might be flexible, due to peering processes and multiple hosting locations for websites. Thus, multiple surfing to the same website, even from the same fixed location, may reach the requested website in servers located in changing parts of the world. Remote interaction, or co-presence, with things, or with appliances located at home, will obviously always reach the same fixed locations, whereas the calling partners may be on the move.

Altogether, then, co-presence with people seems to be the most demanding one, as far as the required coordination, and the involved senses, are concerned. However, at the same time, it is also the most flexible one spatially, in terms of the locations of the parties involved. The meeting of people is mostly an 'active' one, involving speech, whereas the meeting, or attending, of events is a rather 'passive' one, implying watching and listening only. Thus, this latter meeting of events is less demanding, in the sense that no speech is required for attendance, but its scheduling is inflexible. The three forms of co-presence, which do not involve the meeting of people, namely with places, information, and things, are by their very nature, much less demanding, in terms of the use of the senses and any required coordination.

Co-presence may be considered as constituting a sub-class of two wider social relations, other than that of presence: *co-existence* and *spatiality*. Co-existence is a social term, which may include also co-presence as a kind of co-existence of specific individuals at a specific point in time. However, co-existence has much wider cultural and political connotations, as compared to co-presence, since it relates to simultaneously existing social relations, and these do not necessarily assume, or require, continuous co-presence for their very existence. Furthermore, co-existence usually relates to wider societal groups or sectors, living side by side with each other along extensive periods of time, and in wider spaces, as compared to the co-presence of specific individuals, possibly, but not necessarily, being simultaneously stationed only ad hoc in specific sites and at certain times.

The second wider term to which co-presence may belong or relate is the geographical term of *spatiality*, and this one too has a wide connotation, defined as '*any* property relating to or occupying space' (Hillis 2006, p. 455). Co-presence, involving several individuals located simultaneously in one or several places has a spatial connotation given the geographical locations of the involved individuals, and this same condition may apply to the case of simultaneous co-presence of a single individual located in both real and virtual spaces, as well. Co-presence has, therefore, its own spatiality, side by side with numerous other human realities and social conditions that present additional modes of spatiality.

5.6.3 Face-to-Face Co-presence

In this, as well as in the following sections, we will focus in more detail on the three major types of co-presence, namely those occurring with people, places and information. Goffman (1963) was probably the first scholar who systematically studied the role and importance of co-presence, claiming that generally: 'copresence renders persons uniquely accessible, available, and subject to one another' (p. 22). Boden and Molotch (1994) took this notion a step further, in their study of the crucial significance of face-to-face meetings for social contact, focusing mainly on business meetings, in what they termed as the *compulsion of proximity*. They further stated that proximity via physical face-to-face co-presence, or via *connected presence*, as Tillema et al. (2010) termed it, is of special importance even if numerous communications media for virtual connectivity are available to their potential users. Thus, for Boden and Molotch (1994) virtual co-presence may serve as a substitute for face-to-face one, only if the latter cannot be achieved. Furthermore, they believed that communications via virtual media might eventually require some supplementary face-to-face meetings in order to deal with the interpretation of the electronic ones. As we will see, these views have been, partially at least, challenged later on, given the advancement and massive adoption of personal communications technologies as of the 2000s.

Physical co-presence was viewed by Boden and Molotch (1994), as well as by Urry (2003b), as the preferred medium for human interaction, because of the richness of continuous and simultaneous spoken and body languages, a combination that is largely unavailable when people communicate through virtual media. Partially though, signal language exists even in telephone calls, when short or long pauses in speech or in responses may have implications for the transmission and meaning of messages. Similarly, signs or icons expressing feelings and gestures are now widely used in chats and e-mails. Still, face-to-face co-presence permits some unique ways of conversation and gesticulation, e.g. when one speaker completes the sentences of another, or through laughter and small talk. Thus, it was found that important conversations are performed face-to-face rather than over the telephone (Tillema et al. 2010).

As we have noted already in the previous chapter, it was for Urry (2002) to extend Boden and Molotch's (1994) notion of the compulsion for proximity, from their main focus on business interaction, to personal social interactions as well, and these may be maintained and fostered over long distances through air travel. Thus, 'virtual and imaginative travel will not simply substitute for corporeal travel since intermittent co-presence appears obligatory for sustaining much social life' (Urry 2002, p. 258). This same logic for the need of 'meetingness' (Urry 2003b) would also deem fit for local and domestic social ties, maintained and fostered more frequently and through terrestrial travel rather than through air one, in order to bring about face-to-face interaction.

Kaufmann (2002, pp. 22–24, 102) differentiated, in this regard, between two forms of human relations for the establishment of co-presence among people: *contiguity* and *connexity*. Contiguity 'relates to the traditional way people relate to one another in a city, town or village and implies density' (p. 22), thus facilitating face-to-face proximity and co-presence, both possibly achieved after pursuing some walking or driving to a point of meeting, or co-presence. Cities offer, in this regard, 'informal co-presences' through cafés, bars, conferences, campuses and the like (Urry 2003b). Alternatively, connexity 'allows the interaction of actors by canceling out spatial distance' (Kaufmann 2002, p. 22). Connexity can be achieved with the use of communications media, by flying, or via fast terrestrial travel. Kaufmann further stated that speed and distance-based connexity have become socially valued in contemporary society, whereas contiguity has become socially devalued (p. 102). However, as it has recently been found, even under the use of electronic communications, local contacts still prevail (Mok et al. 2010). In the past, though, being *on the road*, or contiguity based on face-to-face co-presences, meant 'progress, stimulation, sophistication, adventure, seeing new places, and exchanging ideas with new acquaintances' (Hanson 1998, p. 242).

It has turned out, already before the introduction, massive development and adoption of Web 2.0 platforms and smartphone applications for social interaction, that the use of virtual communications media may reduce physical, face-to-face contacts (Gershuny 2003; Macdonald and Grieco 2007). This applies mainly to the maintenance of existing and rather strong ties, whereas new and weaker ones would still need physical proximity and co-presence for their fostering and preservation

(Larsen et al. 2006). Generally, though, all forms of interaction and travel were found to be 'of *similar* importance and interconnected with each other' (Larsen et al. 2006, p. 279), and these observations may have remained valid even under the contemporary trend of the massive adoption of virtual social interaction channels, such as Facebook, Twitter, Viber, and WhatsApp. Thus, for instance, given the richness of contact associated with face-to-face meetings by their very nature, real space 'still retains a vital role in contemporary economic and social life' (Warf 2013, p. 147). In addition, it has been evident that 'the more Internet contact, the more in person and phone contact', among both family members and friends (Rainie and Wellman 2012, p. 127).

Under normal conditions, routine daily life for people implies numerous and continuous face-to-face co-presences, taking place at work, at leisure and, in most cases at home too. Less routine face-to-face encounters occur at special occasions, such as in conferences, retreats, and parties, some of which may be initiated by work places, side by side with family meetings marking special events, such as holidays, weddings, etc. (Urry 2002).

5.6.4 Synchronous and Asynchronous Telepresences

The notion of telepresence in its basic connotation refers to the simultaneous presence of at least two individuals, located in their respective physical locations, side by side with their engagement with a virtual location. This latter virtual location, in the case of a communications session, constitutes either of the space 'in between' the interacting parties, as in telephone or online interactions, or of a virtual space accessed through a website (see e.g. Steuer 1992; Miller 2011, pp. 31, 32).

From an experiential perspective, telepresence may relate to some personal sensing experienced by media users: 'the psychological state or subjective perception in which a person fails to accurately and completely acknowledge the role of technology in an experience' (Lombard and Jones 2007, p. 198). Such an experience depends on the levels of *vividness* of the virtual audiovisual session, side by side with the degree of its *interactivity*, or the ability of individuals to influence the content and form of the virtual environment in which they are engaged (Steuer 1992; see also Miller 2011). A studied example in this regard is the online sharing of written, oral and visual experiences by packpackers with friends and family located elsewhere worldwide, thus turning them into flashpackers (e.g. Germann-Molz and Morris-Paris 2015; Mascheroni 2007).

Wellman (2001) outlined several phases in the process of change, which has evolved in the conduct of social relations, following the adoption of transportation and communications technologies, and each of these phases was typified by different patterns of co-presence. The first phase of social relations was defined as the traditional and non-technological *door-to-door* communications of people, for instance when walking for visits with each other, visits which obviously constitute face-to-face co-presence. This type of communications required *synchronous presence* (or co-presence) of the communicating parties in a jointly attended location in real space (Yu and Shaw 2008). A special form of synchronous co-presence is telephone communications among bikers, attempting physical closeness and co-mobility with each other (Mcilvenny 2015).

The automobile and the telephone have permitted the development of a second phase of social relations, as well as of co-presence, namely *place-to-place* ones, offering some flexibility in the location of people's social relations, and thus partially replacing the local door-to-door relations. Place-to-place communications and co-presence consisted, therefore, of both face-to-face ones in real space using cars, side by side with virtual ones, over the telephone. Communications and co-presence via telephones were termed as *connected presence* (Tillema et al. 2010), or 'disembodied sounds—of speech displaced in space and time from its origins' (Mitchell 1995, p. 36), in a kind of 'in between' virtual space. These communications and co-presences were further termed as *synchronous tele-presence* (or co-presence) (Yu and Shaw 2008).

The two media of automobiles and telephones presented several features of contacting. The automobile made it possible for people to reduce their friction of distance drastically, thus permitting additional face-to-face contacts. The fixed line telephone fully nullified the friction of distance, sometimes at high calling rates at the time, thus permitting a rather limited transmission of information, while requiring strict locational co-presence of the interacting parties, for the performance of conversations without any face-to-face contacts (Kellerman 2006a).

Later in the second phase of social relations, the introduction of the Internet has enhanced place-to-place relations and co-presences from its outset, through the provision for the co-presences of users in fixed physical locations, side by side with their locations in virtual spaces, while engaged in Internet activity (see e.g. Kaufmann 2002, p. 28; Urry 2000, p. 71). This co-presence was referred to as simultaneous embodied and response presences (Knorr-Cetina and Bruegger 2002).

Internet communications presented a different mode of communications as compared to the telephone. Internet written communications, notably e-mailing, is both locationally and temporally flexible, since it does not require the synchronous attendance of the communicating parties. Internet written offline communications constitute, therefore, *asynchronous telepresence* (Yu and Shaw 2008), and, it does not imply co-presence. However, Internet online written, audial or audio-visual chats still constitute enhanced synchronous telepresence and co-presence, similarly to those originally facilitated by the telephone.

The most significant contribution of the Internet to new patterns of co-presence has emerged through the introduction of laptops (and later on also tablets), followed by the innovation and wide adoption of smartphones, since both devices permit wireless, and thus placeless, communications, implying the emergence of a third phase in social networking, namely that of *person-to-person* communications. In this type of synchronous telepresence or co-presence, the communicating parties can be detached from any fixed locations for communications media, their related infrastructures and their wired networks.

Licoppe (2004) described the contemporary variety of communications media from a spatiotemporal perspective, as ranging from delayed response (SMS, e-mail, offline chats), through co-presence in time only (telephone, online chatting), to time-space co-presence (face-to-face and virtual audio-visual meetings). This rather wide current availability of varied personal information technologies has turned co-presence more complex. The physically mobile use of smartphones has made it more difficult to identify distinctively co-presence, in the sense of its being simultaneous embodied and response presences, notably from the perspective of users. Still, however, and despite of the wide adoption of personal electronic media which permit virtual co-presence, 'meetingness through co-present bodies seems constitutive of what people experience as the good life 'at-a-distance" (Urry 2002, p. 171).

5.6.5 Co-presence of Physical and Virtual Spaces

Our discussions in the two previous sections focused on face-to-face and remote co-presences of people, at least two of them, located simultaneously in real and virtual spaces. An additional pattern of co-presence involves just one person, exposed simultaneously to her/his location in real space, side by side with their exposure to a single or to several virtual spaces via a website. Such exposures to virtual spaces may take two forms: obligations to places or face-to place communications, implying virtual travel, for instance in order to attend some event, or in order to visit/watch pictures of a remotely located city (Urry 2002). Alternatively, users are exposed to virtual spaces when they perform daily operations through virtual action spaces rather than in real space (Kellerman 2014). The meeting of places in the form of virtual travel and remote attendance of events typified already the early Internet as of its public launching in 1994, whereas the use of the Internet as a second action space for a variety of social and economic activities has typified the more mature Internet developing as of the 2000s.

The meeting of places over the Internet may mean an involvement in travel online, normally constituting preparatory steps towards real space travel, with travel online permitting sophisticated choice processes of vacation destinations. Alternatively, travel online may constitute travel *per se*, either as virtual pleasure travel, and/or as virtual study of places via the Internet. de Botton (2002) called these latter types of virtual travel 'armchair travel', suggesting that 'we may best be able to inhabit a place when we are not faced with the additional challenge of having to be there' (p. 23; see also Urry 2002, n. 18).

The contemporary Internet permits its users to carry out a wide variety of activities through it, activities that could be previously performed only in real space. Leading among these activities are social networking, banking, shopping, travel reserving, interaction with governments, and studying (Kellerman 2014). Internet users tend to perform daily activities through varied combinations between real and virtual spaces, such as touching and trying products in real stores and then purchasing them online or vice versa (see e.g. Schwanen et al. 2008). In all of these activities, the user is exposed to virtual spaces, such as metaphorical governmental offices or bank branches, without regard to the physical location of the servers that host the websites with which interactions take place. Thus, the recent maturing of the virtual Internet space into a space that permits users to perform a wide-range of operations within it, turns the relationships between physical and virtual spaces more diversified and complex. Hence, users might routinely be co-present in a variety of virtual spaces, such as the websites of numerous stores, while still using the same mobile computers (laptops, tablets or smartphones) at home or at work for their access. However, the opposite is also possible now: Internet users may be routinely located in numerous real spaces throughout the day, while interacting with the same virtual spaces, such as their banks, with the use of the same smartphones, even while being on the road.

The use of the Internet for social networking involves the exposure of users not only to virtual spaces but to geographically more dispersed social ties as well, and these rather remote ties may potentially be associated with some erosion of attachment to physical locations, or an increased *placelessness* (see e.g. Relph 1976; Dodge and Kitchin 2001; Wellman 2001; Chap. 3). More generally, the construction of websites for the performance of activities once preserved for real space, and their routine use by Internet subscribers, does not only imply co-presence for their users, but it may further bring about the potential emergence of numerous possible relationships between the two spaces, in their roles as action spaces for daily activities of individuals. First, *competition* between the two spaces; second, *complementarity* between them; third, *substitution* of the real by the virtual; fourth, *escape* from the physical to the virtual; fifth, *merger* of the two spaces; and finally sixth, and theoretically at least, *exclusivity* of activities to be performed in virtual spaces only (for a detailed discussion see Kellerman 2014).

5.6.6 Co-presence in Information Space

As we discussed earlier, in Chap. 2, information space consists of a variety of digital information sets, located within websites or within other digital frameworks, such as data archives, books, articles, documents, or library catalogues (Fabrikant and Buttenfield 2001; Couclelis 1998; Kellerman 2007). These information sets are normally textual and/or graphic, and they have some constancy in terms of their coding, thus making them virtually available to users, and permitting their recalling. Numerous users can share many of these information files: either the public through the Internet, or segmented and permitted users through Intranets.

Co-presence in information space normally involves a single user located in real space and exposed simultaneously to some information source located in cyber-space. Exposures to virtual information sources may vary in form, from the users' perspectives. They may constitute exposures to website offerings, which we discussed before, such as online shopping, paralleling shopping in real space stores. At yet another sphere, readers may be exposed to books and articles paralleling printed editions for these books or articles. Another virtual informational experience can be the exposure of a reader of cyberspatial informational materials to several informational resources simultaneously, something which is equivalent to two or more printed books being open in front of a reader in real space.

The difference between the simultaneous availabilities of multiple informational resources in real space, as compared to those in virtual spaces, is the level of sophistication and speed of information manipulation available for readers of digital materials, e.g. the use of search engines, comparison of sources, copying, etc. The very ability of readers to save digital materials, as well as to 'cut and paste' within them, is not novel, since such abilities have been available also for printed materials, but these actions could be performed with printed materials in more restricted and rather cumbersome ways, as compared to those available in informational space. Work in information space attempts to imitate readers' actions that are well known to them from real space, through the adoption of metaphorical terms, such as 'open', 'save', 'merge', 'cut', 'paste', etc. Thus, the co-presence of one or several cyberspatial information sources implies for their readers the creation of a virtual office or lab spaces for students, scholars or professional workers who are co-present in real space.

5.6.7 Multiple Simultaneous Co-presences

An ultimate scenario of co-presence complexity can be a scenario that involves two or more people located in different time zones, interacting through some chat platform, while all of them being also simultaneously involved in other, virtual or real space activities. For example, one of them consulting several information sources, another one being involved in some online activity, such as shopping, and a third one being on travel. Scenarios like this one, as well as other similar multiple simultaneous co-presences, have become possible through contemporary advancements in the speed of information transmissions, the full mobility and access of information provided by smartphones, and above all, the very readiness of people to be engaged in complex co-presence conditions.

Another transition bearing upon co-presences of individuals is the blurring of the traditional distinction between home and work, in a world of enhanced communications technologies. These two most basic fixities or locations of individuals were traditionally assigned with distinct activities to be performed in each of them. Contemporarily, however, work-related activities frequently interrupt home ones, and the other way around (see Kellerman 2006a). Such multi-tasking implies co-presences, which individuals might experience, sometimes unwillingly so, as they are forced into them implicitly or explicitly by their employers, who assume a permanent exposure of workers to the Internet via PCs, smartphones, laptops and tablets (see Kaufmann 2002, p. 28; Urry 2000, p. 71). Such multiple co-presences are mostly noted at home, to a degree of turning the home into a 'terminal' (Urry 2000, p. 72). In addition, dwelling itself has been considered as becoming impermanent and mobile, so that homes are sometimes considered as locations rather than as places, side by side with communities which have been based on geographical proximity among their residents, and are becoming now dependent upon varied patterns of mobilities (Urry 2000, pp. 141, 144, 157).

Multiple co-presences may emerge also while driving. Katz (1999, pp. 35, 36) noted, for instance, that when a driver becomes involved in a telephone conversation, the double activity of driving and calling implies that she/he is simultaneously involved in co-presence at two distinct social settings: fellow car drivers sharing a specific route, and the partner of the phone conversation. Such a double co-presence may imply that when traffic slows down, or at times of other road and traffic disturbances, drivers may become angry, since such disturbances may lead to increased involvement in the changing driving conditions, at the expense of the degree of their involvement in their phone conversation.

5.6.8 Co-presence in the City

Urbanites can be classified, from a communications perspective, as being, at any point in time, engaged in some form of co-presence. One form of such an urban co-presence could be termed as passive presence, referring, as we mentioned already, to a condition of somebody being located next to fellow urbanites in a public or semi-public domain, while not being engaged in face-to-face conversation with those others. Another urban co-presence pattern is an active one, implying involvement in interaction with one or more physically present partners. A third type of urban co-presence is the virtual one, when individuals are located in the public spheres of cities while making use of mobile phones and similar devices there (Kopomaa 2000).

The permanent occurrence of virtual co-presences has turned the urban co-presence landscape more diversified and complex. Thus, people located in urban public spaces are increasingly more involved in mobile telephone calls, or in website surfing, while physically located in the public sphere. Such virtual co-presence by individuals occurs side by side with fellow urbanites being involved simultaneously in passive and active face-to-face co-presence in urban public spaces. More and more people engage in telephone calls while walking on the streets, standing in line, riding public transportation, or when driving their cars. Similarly, more and more people make use of the Internet through laptops and tablets, or through smartphones, while sitting in a park or in a café, possibly using Wi-Fi connectivity. Other people may occasionally interrupt a face-to-face conversation because of incoming phone calls. Urry (2007, p. 176) termed this multiple scene of communications and co-presence as *connectivity*, thus emphasizing that people tend to get engaged in the use of mobile communications media while being involved in corporeal mobility through walking, riding or driving, or while waiting for a ride on a public transportation medium. Hence, places themselves seem as traveling (Urry 2004).

Virtual co-presence activities of urbanites do not automatically interfere with those performed by fellow urbanites, all of whom sharing the same open area, unless there is some communications traffic congestion due to restricted wireless bandwidth. In addition, telephone callers in public areas may control their virtual co-presence for a minimization of nuisances, possibly being caused to fellow users of the public urban sphere, for example by using earphones, and by talking in low voice in their telephone conversations.

5.6.9 Contemporary Co-presence Modes

The contemporary variety and complexity of possibilities for co-presence, which we have discussed so far, is quite novel. It has begun with the gradual household adoption of telephones as of the early twentieth century, and it has culminated with the wide and fast adoption of the Internet, coupled later with sophisticated mobile communications devices, as of the late twentieth century. Before the introduction of personal information technologies, co-presence was mainly restricted to face-to-face meetings among people, with even more restricted co-presence patterns of people with places, for instance when they were looking at printed pictures and maps, and later on at a higher level of co-presence, when watching movies. The introduction and adoption of the Internet, and even more so the adoption of mobile communications, has opened up a variety of novel virtual encounters, possibly led by the possibility to use cyber information space, which has brought about new patterns of co-presence.

Interestingly enough, the swift emergence of new modes of co-presence has made them become part of our routine daily conduct, as if they have always been there as part of our 'natural' life. This easy adoption of new co-presence modes is even more striking with regard to young children who accept and live easily with several modes of co-presence as of early childhood. One major implication of the experiencing of extensive co-presences is the blurring between 'here' and 'there'. The introduction and adoption of chatting rooms and blogs in the 1990s made partner B in an exchange wonder what was the meaning of partner A in her/his claiming 'I'm here'. Did this refer to their physical location or to their virtual availability? The more recent introduction of numerous avenues for virtual reaching out and the exposures of individuals not just to fellow people, but also to places, events and information, have made users themselves, or their partner in an interaction, wonder where they are when engaged in virtual co-presences: whether in real space, in virtual one, or somewhere 'in between'. These emerging transitions in the meanings of personal locations may continue to develop if future information technologies, such as 3D (three-dimensional) communications, will call for them. Such transitions may potentially lead, in the near or far future, to transitions in the very connotation and definition of presence, not just that of co-presence.

Traditional co-presence required locational fixity for its very occurrence in face-to-face meetings, whereas the availability of mobile devices has turned co-presence into something being continuously on the move. Moreover, it is now possible, with the pressing of a single virtual button to move from one type of co-presence, for instance among people, to another one, e.g. between a user and information. It is also possible for individuals to be engaged in two types of co-presence simultaneously, when a screen is shared between two types of reaching out, such as with people and information. Thus, the very differentiation among the numerous types of co-presence may blur, potentially at least, turning them all into co-presence as just a single, and rather general, class, stemming from reaching out, again as a single and general class. The standard software employed now by individual Internet users worldwide for co-presence options may enhance this latter possibility of single-class reaching out and its associated single-class co-presence. Software packages and applications such as Windows, Office, Google, Facebook and Twitter, may lead such a trend. These globally used commercial tools may contribute to an emergence of similar co-presence operation modes and respectively their similar experiencing by people of different cultures worldwide.

The Internet of things still awaits its full introduction and adoption, eventually bringing about the remote control and operation of household devices. As for the veteran types of co-presence, the information technology (IT) industry is currently involved in an ongoing technological effort to enhance the screen quality of communications devices, notably through the provision of higher density of pixels, thus producing sharper screens. Another technological effort involves the development of three- dimensional (3D) screens. Upgraded visual interfaces for users with fellow people, places, events, and even with information, may imply more realistic virtual co-presence experiences, thus turning virtual co-presence experiences more significant. Among the several attractions/stimuli for co-presence, enhanced visualities on computer screens might be something of special importance, particularly for inter-personal co-presences.

5.7 Time-Space Compression

The use of the notion of time-space compression dates back to transportation geographers in the 1950s and 1960s, but the idea of time and space shrinking has earlier roots (Warf 2011). Time-space compression was defined, within the context of geographical social theory, as the 'compression of our spatial and temporal worlds' (Harvey 1989, p. 240), thus constituting a 'pull' mechanism, induced by contemporary telecommunications technologies. Originally, time-space compression was proposed for rather macro societal trends and developments. Thus, time-space compression was attributed to global capitalism and as well as to the growing speeds for the movements of capital and business people, coupled with growing inequalities, pertaining to groups of people who lead processes of time-space compression, others who enjoy them, and additional groups who are left behind (Massey 2008, p. 259).

Time-space compression may as well emerge and be the case for wide individual interactions and experiences within 'Internet time' and 'electronic space' (Tsatsou 2009). Thus, time-space compression may accompany global social interactions carried out by individuals, for example among members of diaspora communities when calling their countries of origin, located in a different time-zone than their current countries of residence (see e.g. Youngstedt 2004). Furthermore, time-space compression may apply also to contemporary global and thus continuous work-related interactions by workers (Kesselring 2015).

Time-space compression is there, for example, when a chat takes place between two parties located in Australia and the UK, respectively. This chat implies that one of the two communicating parties may be awake late at night, or working at that time, so that both time and space differences between the two parties and their locations have been compressed in the parties' online interaction. Time-space compression for individuals may be viewed as an effect of co-presence in the special case of long-distance interaction with people. The degree of time-space compression of Internet users in general, and of those active in global networks in particular, may be easily measured through the temporal patterns of their communications sessions.

Time-space compression may constitute a matter of choice in some of people's social interactions with friends or family members located, permanently or temporarily, in other parts of the world. However, time-space compression may also mean a hardship for Internet users in numerous other cases. For social communications, this may be the case, when some family members were forced to migrate to another part of the world, while keeping in touch with their family remaining in their countries of origin. Even more so, in the work sphere, workers may be forced, explicitly or implicitly, to interact with colleagues in other parts of the world, sometimes on a routine basis. Such a constraint on daily life may divide workers and jobs within companies between those that permit full night sleep and those that do not. This constitutes a class-division among workers, similarly, for example, to the differentiation among those who make wide use of the Internet, thus being permanently virtually mobile, whereas others have to take care of its maintenance, and thus being more fixed in space (see e.g. Massey 1993; Cresswell 2001).

5.8 Conclusion

In this chapter, we focused on elements of mobility and their operations in cyberspace, thus exploring terms that have been proposed within the study of mobilities, notably those related to personal mobilities. We presented, first, the notion of cyber-mobility, referring to the very mobility of people through the Internet, followed by discussions of six specific mobility notions: flow, speed, directionality, circularity, co-presence, and time-space compression.

Cyber-mobility constitutes the mobility of information, of all types and for all purposes, through the cyberspatial Internet. Cyber-mobility has become increasingly significant along the gradual introduction of technological innovations permitting faster information transmissions, culminating with mobile broadband for smartphones. Thus, personal mobilities about cities involve simultaneously real and virtual mobilities, bringing about a decreasing experiencing of urban landscapes.

Flows of information were considered as being flexible as the movements of gas, and flows within the Internet were viewed like fluids of social relations, with varying degrees of freedom of movements, depending on the type of networks. Flows for individuals in cyberspatial contexts refer to the flows of information along screen sequences, as well as to the flows of the interactions of users with websites, notably with service oriented ones. Flows can, thus, be measured by the rate of unsuccessful completions of transactions per website, and/or by the time it takes for the completion of successful ones.

Speed, as expressed in the contemporary urgencies for immediacy and instantaneity, has led to the growing contemporary rush for the production and consumption of increasing fixed and mobile broadband Internet speeds, mainly in developed countries. These faster speeds have permitted to turn the Internet into service and entertainment action spaces, on the demand side, side by side with their facilitation of production landscapes in websites for business, on the supply side. Broadband speed availabilities differ among countries, as well as among specific places and given times of use. These speeds can be measured through the ping utility.

Directionality, or predefined geographical destinations, typifies most movements in physical space, but this is mostly not the case for cyberspatial movements. In the communications space of the Internet, messages are geared for people, who may retrieve them with their mobile communications devices anywhere in real space. Similarly, in both information searches and in surfing to specific websites, users are interested in the contents of consulted websites and in the identity of their owners, but not in the changing geographical locations in physical space of the servers that host them. Generally then, cyberspatial directionality refers to Internet destinations, namely people in the communications space, and websites or information, in the information space. The real space locations for these destinations seem irrelevant in most cases. It is still possible, though, to trace the location of reached servers through some specific tracing tools.

Circularity of movements constitute the usual case for Internet users who return normally to their home page at the end of their use sessions. However, Internet surfing sessions may not just consist of the reaching of a single destination, but they may involve surfing to numerous websites sequentially. In addition, some Internet use sessions may frequently be cyclical, for instance, when the same website is being used periodically. Both the circularity and the cyclicality of Internet use sessions can be simply measured by noting the specific websites from which surfing begins, the websites visited during any session, and the website in which sessions conclude.

We paid detailed attention to co-presence, given its being an experience that is there for all uses of the Internet. We have noted a wide variety of co-presence scenarios, emerging when individuals reach out to all five possible types of attractions or communications stimuli: fellow people, places, events, information, and things. Co-presence is obviously also the case when Internet users are engaged in combinations among these attractions, notably within urban contexts. Reaching out virtually through co-presence involves particular functions and patterns attributed to each of the attractions that may bring it about. Mobile phones, tablets and laptops, permit people's engagement in location-free extensive virtual co-presences.

We further noted the wide assessment of virtual co-presences as being less significant experiences than those attained in real space face-to-face ones. Still, it is important to note that the contemporary information age has provided for an impressive variety of opportunities for co-presence through communications technologies that facilitate personal mobility, with people enjoying the continuous availability of these personal communications devices. Thus, contemporary individuals in the developed world experience co-presence much more extensively than just a decade or two ago, but these virtual co-presence experiences maybe shallower in their very experiencing and imprints, as compared to face-to-face ones in real space. Even under these circumstances of growing mobile communications, cities have kept their feature as foci for co-presences, albeit involving now simultaneous face-to-face and virtual ones, in public as well as in private urban spheres.

Time-space compression may emerge in global social interactions by individuals, as well as in both domestic and global, and thus continuous, work-related interactions by workers. The degree of time-space compression of Internet users may be easily measured through the timings of their communications sessions.

The six parameters that we examined in this chapter apply differentially to the information and communications spheres of the Internet, as well as to the Internet in general. Thus, flows are relevant for website uses, or the information space of the Internet, mainly for the convenience of screen sequences. Speeds of transmission are also of importance for the sequences of website screens or pages. In the communications space speed is of significance mainly for video calls. Cyberspatial directionality exists in both the communications and information spheres of the Internet, referring to Internet destinations of people and information, respectively, but not to their locations in real space. Circularity, or a return at the end of sessions to the starting point, the homepage, seems to be the case in information space activities, some of which are also cyclical, thus preformed at specific repetitive times. Co-presence applies, by definition, to all the uses or interactions performed through the Internet, whether with people, through the communications space, or with the numerous types of information, accessed and used through websites. Finally, time-space compression may take place in long-distance online communications offered by the Internet communications space.

References

Amin, A., & Thrift, N. (2002). *Cities: Reimagining the Urban*. Cambridge: Polity.

Arminen, I. (2007). Review essay: mobile communication society? *Acta Sociologica, 50*, 431–437.

Avidan, I., & Kellerman, A. (2004). Distance in the Internet by time and route: An empirical examination. *Horizons (Contemporary Israeli Geography), 60–61*, 77–88.

Baumann, Z. (2003). *Liquid love: On the frailty of human bonds*. Cambridge: Polity Press.
Boden, D., & Molotch, H. L. (1994). The compulsion of proximity. In R. Friedland & D. Boden (Eds.), *Nowhere space, time and modernity* (pp. 257–286). Berkeley: University of California Press.
Bonss, W., & Kesselring, S. (2004). *Mobility and the cosmopolitan perspective*. Munich: The mobility and the cosmopolitan perspective workshop Reflexive Modernization Research Centre. http://www.mobilitypioneers.de/Dokumente/download/November%202004/B3_Workshop_0104_Dokumentation.pdf.
COPC (2016). copc.com.
Couclelis, H. (1998). Worlds of information: The geographic metaphor in the visualization of complex information. *Cartography and Geographic Information Systems, 25*, 209–220.
Cresswell, T. (2001). The production of mobilities. *New. Formations, 43*, 11–25.
de Botton, A. (2002). *The art of travel*. London: Hamish Hamilton.
De Certeau, M. (1985). Practices of space. In M. Blonsky (Ed.), *On Signs* (pp. 122–145). Oxford: Basil Blackwell.
Dodge, M., & Kitchin, R. (2001). *Mapping cyberspace*. London: Routledge.
Emerson, T., Steed, A. & Billinghurst, M. (1999). *Presence Bibliography*. University of Washington Human Interface Laboratory (HitLab), Technical Publication R-99-9. http://www.hitl.washington.edu/publications/r-99-9/.
Fabrikant, S. I., & Buttenfield, B. P. (2001). Formalizing semantic spaces for information access. *Annals of the Association of American Geographers, 91*, 263–280.
Farman, J. (2012). *Mobile interface theory: Embodied space and locative media*. London and New York: Routledge.
Freund, P., & Martin, G. (1993). *The ecology of the automobile*. Montreal: Black Rose Books.
Gergen, K. (2002). The challenge of absent presence. In J. Katz & M. Aakhus (Eds.), *Perpetual contact* (pp. 227–241). Cambridge: Cambridge University Press.
Germann-Molz, J., & Morris-Paris, C. (2015). The social affordances of flashpacking: Exploring the mobility nexus of travel and communication. *Mobilities, 10*, 173–192.
Gershuny, J. (2003). Web use and net nerds: A neofunctionalist analysis of the impact of information technology in the home. *Social Forces, 82*, 141–168.
Goffman, E. (1963). *Behavior in public places: Notes on the social organization of gatherings*. New York: Free Press.
Goffman, E. (1971). *Relations in public: Microstudies of the public order*. Harmondsworth: Penguin.
Hägerstrand, T. (1970). What about people in regional science? *Papers and Proceedings of the Regional Science Association, 24*, 7–21.
Hägerstrand, T. (1973). The domain of human geography. In R. J. Chorley (Ed.), *Directions in Geography* (pp. 67–87). London: Methuen.
Hägerstrand, T. (1975). Space, time and human conditions. In A. Karlqvist, L. Lundqvist, & F. Snickers (Eds.), *Allocation of Urban space* (pp. 3–12). Farnborough: Saxon House.
Hägerstrand, T. (1992). Mobility and transportation—are economics and technology the only limits? *Facta and Futura, 2*, 35–38.
Hanson, S. (1998). Off the road? Reflections on transportation geography in the information age. *Journal of Transport Geography, 6*, 241–249.
Harvey, D. (1989). *The condition of postmodernity*. Oxford: Blackwell.
Hillis, K. J. (2006). Spatiality. In B. Warf (Ed.), *Encyclopedia of Human Geography* (p. 455). Thousand Oaks, CA: Sage.
IJsselsteijn, W. A., Lombard, M., & Freeman, J. (2001). Toward a core bibliography of presence. *Cyberpsychology and Behavior, 4*, 317–321.
ITU (International Telecommunication Union) (2015). ICT Facts and Figures: The World in 2015. http://www.itu.int/en/ITU-D/Statistics/Pages/stat/default.aspx.
Katz, J. (1999). *How emotions work*. Chicago: The University of Chicago Press.
Kaufmann, V. (2002). *Re-thinking mobility: Contemporary sociology*. Aldershot: Ashgate.
Kellerman, A. (1993). *Telecommunications and Geography*. London: Belhaven (Wiley).

Kellerman, A. (1999). Leading nations in the adoption of communications media 1975–1995. *Urban Geography, 20*, 377–389.

Kellerman, A. (2006a). *Personal mobilities*. London and New York: Routledge.

Kellerman, A. (2006b). Broadband penetration and its implications: The case of France. *Netcom, 20*, 237–246.

Kellerman, A. (2007). Cyberspace classification and cognition: Information and communications cyberspaces. *Journal of Urban Technology, 14*, 5–32.

Kellerman, A. (2012). *Daily spatial mobilities: Physical and virtual*. Farnham: Ashgate.

Kellerman, A. (2014). *The internet as second action space*. London and New York: Routledge.

Kesselring, S. (2015). Corporate mobilities regimes. Mobility, power and the socio-geographical structurations of mobile work. *Mobilities, 10*, 571–591.

Kesselring, S., & Vogl, G. (2004). *Mobility pioneers: Networks, scapes and flows between first and second modernity*. Munich: The mobility and the cosmopolitan perspective workshop Reflexive Modernization Research Centre. http://citeseerx.ist.psu.edu/viewdoc/download?doi=10.1.1.196.3277&rep=rep1&type=pdf.

Kitchin, R., & Dodge, M. (2011). *Code/space: Software and everyday life*. Cambridge: MIT Press.

Knorr-Cetina, K., & Bruegger, U. (2002). Global microstructures: The virtual societies of financial markets. *American Journal of Sociology, 107*, 905–950.

Kopomaa, T. (2000). *The city in your pocket: Birth of the mobile information society*. Helsinki: Gaudeamus.

Kwan, M.-P. (2001). Cyberspatial cognition and individual access to information: The behavioral foundation of cybergeography. *Environment and Planning B, 28*, 21–37.

Larsen, J., Axhausen, K. W., & Urry, J. (2006). Geographies of social networks: Meetings, travel and communications. *Mobilities, 1*, 261–283.

Lee, K. M. (2004). Presence, explicated. *Communication Theory, 14*, 27–50.

Licoppe, C. (2004). 'Connected' presence: The emergence of a new repertoire for managing social relationships in a changing communication technoscape. *Environment and Planning D: Society and Space, 22*, 135–156.

Ling, R. (2008). *New tech, new ties*. Cambridge: MIT Press.

Lombard, M., & Jones, M. T. (2007). Identifying the (tele)presence literature. *PsychNology, 5*, 197–206.

Macdonald, K., & Gieco, M. (2007). Accessibility, mobility and connectivity: The changing frontiers of everyday routine. *Mobilities, 2*, 1–14.

Mascheroni, G. (2007). Global nomads' network and mobile sociality. *Information, Communication & Society, 10*, 527–546.

Massey, D. (1993). Power-geometry and a progressive sense of place. In J. Bird, B. Curtis, T. Putnam, G. Robertson, & L. Tickner (Eds.), *Mapping the futures: Local cultures, global change* (pp. 59–69). London: Routledge.

Massey, D. (2008). A global sense of place. In T. S. Oakes & P. L. Price (Eds.), *The cultural Geography reader* (pp. 257–263). London & New York: Routledge.

Mcilvenny, P. (2015). The joy of biking together: Sharing everyday experiences of vélomobility. *Mobilities, 10*, 55–82.

Miller, V. (2011). *Understanding digital culture*. London: Sage.

Mitchell, W. J. (1995). *City of bits: Space, place, and the Infobahn*. Cambridge: MIT Press.

Mok, D., Wellman, B., & Carrasco, J. (2010). Does distance matter in the age of the Internet? *Urban Studies, 47*, 2747–2783.

Neotrace (2015). Extremely fast traceroute program. http://neotrace-pro.en.softonic.com/.

Oxford Reference (2015). Co-presence. http://www.oxfordreference.com/view/10.1093/oi/authority.20110803095638654.

Pearce, P. & Gretzel, U. (2012). Tourism in technology dead zones: Documenting experiential dimensions. *International Journal of Tourism Sciences*, 12, 1–20.

Rainie, L., & Wellman, B. (2012). *Networked: The new social operating system*. Cambridge: MIT Press.

Relph, E. (1976). *Place and placelessness*. London: Pion.

Schubert, T. W. (2009). A new conception of spatial presence: Once again, with feeling. *Communication Theory, 19*, 161–187.
Schwanen, T., Dijst, M., & Kwan, M.-P. (2008). ICTs and the decoupling of everyday activities, space and time: Introduction. *Tijdschrift voor Economische en Sociale Geografie, 9*, 519–527.
Sheller, M. (2004). Mobile publics: Beyond the network perspective. *Environment and Planning D: Society and Space, 22*, 39–52.
Skarauskiene, A., & Kalinauskas, M. (2015). The Internet of things: When reality meets expectations. *International Journal of Innovation and Learning, 17*, 262–274.
Steuer, J. (1992). Defining virtual reality: Dimensions determining telepresence. *Journal of Communication, 4*, 73–93.
Tillema, T., Dijst, M., & Schwanen, T. (2010). Decisions concerning communication modes and the influence of travel time: A situational approach. *Environment and Planning A, 42*, 2058–2077.
Time (2015). Go to Europe if you want fast mobile Internet. http://time.com/3744133/country-fastest-mobile-broadband/. (13 March).
Tsatsou, P. (2009). Reconceptualising 'time' and 'space' in the era of electronic media and communications. *PLATFORM: Journal of Media and Communication, 1*, 11–32.
Urry, J. (2000). *Sociology beyond Societies: Mobilities for the Twenty-first Century*. London: Routledge.
Urry, J. (2002). Mobility and proximity. *Sociology, 36*, 255–274.
Urry, J. (2003a). *Global complexity*. Cambridge: Polity.
Urry, J. (2003b). Social networks, travel and talk. *British Journal of Sociology, 54*, 155–175.
Urry, J. (2004). The 'system' of automobility. *Theory, Culture and Society, 21*, 25–39.
Urry, J. (2007). *Mobilities*. Cambridge: Polity Press.
Virilio, P. (1977). *Vitesse et Politique*. Paris: Galilee.
Virilio, P. (1983). *Pure war*. New York: Semiotext(e)..
Warf, B. (2011). Excavating the prehistory of time-space compression. *The Geographical Review, 101*, 435–446.
Warf, B. (2013). *Global Geographies of the internet*. Dordrecht: Springer.
Wellman, B. (2001). Physical place and cyberplace: The rise of personalized networking. *International Journal of Urban and Regional Research, 25*, 227–252.
Youngstedt, S. M. (2004). The new Nigerian Hausa diaspora in the US: Surviving and building community on the margins of the global economy. *City and Society, 16*, 39–67.
Yu, H., & Shaw, S.-L. (2008). Exploring potential human activities in physical and virtual spaces: A spatio-temporal GIS approach. *International Journal of Geographical Information Science, 22*, 409–430.

Chapter 6
Internet Spatial Cognition

Abstract In this chapter, the veteran notions of spatial cognition and cognitive maps, developed originally for real space, are examined for the Internet and its two classes of information and communications spaces. Whereas for real space, space and its maps are two completely separate entities, in informational cyberspace they actually converge. Internal and external mapping seem irrelevant for cognitive communications space.

Keywords Cognitive information space · Cognitive communications space

The veteran notions of *cognitive space* and *cognitive/mental maps* were proposed already back in the late 1940s, and they have been extensively studied as of the 1970s, within behavioral geography, as well as within tangent disciplines, notably environmental psychology and architecture. These two notions assumed space as constituting a personally experienced real space, producing a variety of individual cognitive experiences, differentiated by the type of the experienced environments. Major examples include the personal experiencing of indoor spaces versus outdoor ones (see e.g., Sommer 1969; Altman 1975), and human exposure to urban spaces, as compared to people's exposures to rural and natural ones (see e.g., Allen 1999).

The introduction and massive adoption of the Internet as of the mid-1990s has brought about a wide exposure of individuals to cyberspace as a type of space, which has implied its possible personal experiencing and cognition, and, thus, the possible yielding of cognitive cyberspaces. As such, cognitive cyberspace cannot be found within cyberspace itself, nor can it be found within real space, as compared to the geographical notions discussed for the Internet in Chaps. 3–5. Rather, cognitive cyberspace is to be found in Internet users' minds, similarly to cognitive real space.

In this chapter, we will attempt to examine cognitive cyberspace, through its classification into the two major classes of cognitive information cyberspace and cognitive communications cyberspace, following our classification of the Internet so far. As we will comment later on, the third possible class of Internet cognitive space, namely cognitive screen space, is included within the other two classes of cognitive cyberspace. Our discussions in this chapter will be based, in part, on

A. Kellerman, *Geographic Interpretations of the Internet*,
SpringerBriefs in Geography, DOI 10.1007/978-3-319-33804-0_6

notions developed elsewhere (Kellerman 2007), and more detailed discussions may be found there. We will begin our discussions with a brief exposition of the general concepts of spatial cognition and cognitive maps.

6.1 Spatial Cognition and Cognitive Maps

When the concepts of spatial cognition and cognitive maps are examined from a geographical perspective, it is possible to identify a process that leads from one's sensing of space through her/his cognitive abilities and processes, leading to the production of subjective and rather internal cognitive maps. We sense and absorb space and geographical information stemming from numerous sources. The first sources are the primary ones, for instance through walking, with landmarks, paths, and scenes, as major elements for the learning and sensing of environments (see e.g., Hochmair and Frank 2001). Second, we absorb geographical information from secondary sources, mainly through maps, pictures, text readings, and communications (Kitchin 2001; Dodge and Kitchin 2001). A third source of geographical information is our spatial cognition, based on previous spatial learnings. This past cognitive experience involves 'the retention, organization, and structuring of spatial information in the mind' (Gale and Golledge 1982, p. 63), and these may eventually lead to a configurational knowledge of specific environments.

Internal cognitive maps can also be externalized on paper, and, thus, are able to attest to personal spatial knowledge and behavior, as well as to societal ones through the aggregation of numerous cognitive maps of the same area. As such, cognitive maps may be considered as subsets of the more general notion of spatial cognition, which we briefly discussed so far (Golledge and Stimson 1997). The quality of externalized cognitive maps depends also on persons' cartographic abilities for map drawing. Cognitive maps were first proposed by Tolman (1948), and were defined as 'a representative expression of an individual's cognitive map knowledge, where cognitive map knowledge is an individual's knowledge about the spatial and environmental relations of geographic space' (Kitchin 2001; see also Kitchin and Blades 2002). Cognitive maps may further represent imagined and not necessarily present environments (Golledge and Stimson 1997). Furthermore, cognitive mapping presents 'a very high level of spatial processing, involving a kind of survey representation of the environment, which makes it possible to move efficiently between the places charted on a map' (Péruch et al. 2000, p. 108).

As we just noted, drawn cognitive maps may attest to individual patterns of spatial behavior (Golledge and Stimson 1997). In addition, the aggregate analyses of numerous cognitive maps all for a specific urban area, focusing on major spatial elements, such as paths, edges, districts, nodes, and landmarks, may tell, among other things, about the aggregate societal knowledge of an area (Lynch 1961). Shum (1990), following Downs and Stea (1973), argued for a functional, rather than a structural, equivalence between cartographic and cognitive maps. Thus, these two map types include both locational and attributional information, and in this feature both map types constitute a transformation process of an object set into an image, since users of a spatial unit or of a cartographic map turn these object sets into images imprinted in them.

Cognitive space may further be viewed as a kind of *personal space*. Originally, the notion of personal space referred to people's need and tendency to maintain a bubble-like invisible and flexible space or distance between them and fellow individuals within changing social settings, as well as within differing spaces of meeting with other people in real space (see Chap. 3). This kind of personal space or spacing is flexible, depending on social circumstances, so that personal space in a crowded bus, for instance, is smaller than in classrooms (Sommer 1969; Altman 1975). However, the term personal space may not only imply space with a connotation of an empty, invisible partition or separation among individuals. Personal space may constitute also a piece of real space, personally designed and used, such as one's home or one's office, or even one's desk. Personal space has an even wider meaning, referring to any personally experienced, and, thus, cognized real spaces (not just real spaces personally designed or used), and these personally experienced spaces yield cognitive maps which people develop in their minds (and which may be put also on paper).

How do the notions of spatial cognition and mental maps, discussed so far, fit the cyberspatial experience of Internet users? We have noted already in Chaps. 1 and 2, that cyberspace constitutes by its very nature a distinct category and entity, as compared to real space. However, the notion of personal space, in the sense of its constitution as any personally experienced and cognized space, might also be relevant for cognitive cyberspaces. Personal cyberspace is, therefore, any experienced and, thus, cognized Internet screen, presenting some pieces of information stemming from the informational or communicative Internet spaces. Thus, Internet screens cannot be recognized as a separate class for cognitive cyberspace, but rather they serve as the medium for users' cognition of information and communication spaces. The basic character of cognitive cyberspace is its constitution of a reflection of the rather virtual cyberspace, as the input or source for the creation of a personal cognitive cyberspace.

We will demonstrate the notion of cognitive cyberspaces through our following separate expositions of the two Internet cognitive spaces, namely information and communications spaces, respectively, both evolving through the visual screen spaces. We will discuss the relations among the three classes of Internet spaces in the next chapter, but will demonstrate in the following two sections, that similarly to individuals' cognition of real space they may cognize the two classes of cyberspace in some distinct ways for each space, through the interface of computer screens.

6.2 Cognitive Information Space

Cognitive information space refers to the cognition of Internet information spaces by its users, focusing on screen presentations of landscapes and maps. The cognition of virtual landscapes by Internet users is normally partial, since Internet surfers see only a visually restricted Web page at a time, and this makes it difficult for them to cognize fully, through a single screen, a complete virtual landscape (Kwan 2001). However, this limitation may be resolved, at least partially, in the future, when new technologies, notably visual 3D technologies, will be fully developed and adopted.

The rather partial cognition of virtual landscapes is further restricted by the probable inability of users to create mental maps of the cognized virtual landscapes following their cognition. Only theoretically, then, if cognitive mapping of virtual landscapes would have been possible, it would have differed from internal and external cognitive maps for real space. The basic difference between these two types of cognitive maps stems from the basic difference between real space and cyberspace. Real space can be experienced bodily and mentally using all the senses. Similarly, cartographic maps drawn for real space territories constitute material paper documents, which are, therefore, stable entities of information. Cyberspace, on the other hand, is a most flexible and instantly changing mode of information presentation, sensed by its users in rather restricted ways, normally visually or audio-visually only, as we noted already in our discussion of screens as ground (Chap. 3).

This major difference between the cognition and mental mapping of real and virtual landscapes and maps, led Kwan (2001, p. 26) to state that mental mapping of virtual landscapes is impossible (based on Golledge (1995, 1999)): 'without the sense of location, distance, and direction necessary for the formation of configurational spatial knowledge, and without a habitual movement pattern essential for developing route-based spatial knowledge, an articulated cognitive map of cyberspace cannot be established.' Internet users may have difficulties to cognize and eventually draw cognitive maps of virtual landscapes or of virtual cartographic maps that they may have been exposed to in restricted sensory ways over the Internet. Furthermore, virtual landscapes or maps can be instantly manipulated in varied ways, mainly through changes made in their scale, size, directions, colors, richness of information, etc., and virtual texts too can be manipulated through changes in their formats, fonts, color, etc. Such manipulations may add to the difficulty to cognize cyberspace presentations in memorable ways. Kwan (2001) noted for real space that space and its maps are two completely separate entities, and as we noted now, in cyberspace they may actually converge.

6.3 Cognitive Communications Space

Cognitive communications was recognized as a metaphorical space, notably for audial telephone conversations, a cognitive cyberspace which merely permits a feeling of 'presence' and intimacy by the communicating parties. As Shields (2003) stated, "the virtual' is imagined as a 'space' between participants, a computer-generated common ground which is neither actual in its location or coordinates, nor is it merely a conceptual abstraction, for it may be experienced 'as if' lived for given purposes' (p. 49). However, cognitive communications cyberspace may constitute more than a purely imagined and metaphorical space, when video calls are made. In such calls cognitive communications space may refer to the real spaces surrounding the two communicating persons who make use of video media for their conversation. These real spaces may be sensed, experienced, or just imagined over the contemporary variety of video communications media. The involvement of a visual live dimension in video communications implies a virtual embodiment and an extended sense of co-presence by the communicating parties (see Chap. 5).

Cognitive communications space differs widely from cognitive aspects relating to face-to-face communications in real space. When two people meet physically, the environment in which their meeting takes place constitutes an integral element of the meeting, and in several ways. Directly, there are sights, lights, smells, weather conditions, and noises, all of which may draw the attention of the meeting parties, since all of their senses are active. Indirectly, the meeting environment may serve or deter the verbal exchanges among the meeting persons, depending on the meeting setting and atmosphere. Thus, for example, a quiet and cozy restaurant may fit certain meetings more than a crowded fast food facility. These surrounding elements of face-to-face meetings are almost absent from virtual video communications. In such calls, each party is located in her/his own physical environment, and the elements that can be seen and heard of the surrounding environment by the called party, through electronic communications, is partial and is perceived as belonging to the separate and unshared physical space of the called party.

Cognitive communications space differs also widely from cognitive space in general, namely for the cognition of real space in circumstances other than face-to-face meetings. Above all, the cognition of real space evolves and nests in one's mind routinely, for the purposes of orientation or navigation in space (Chang 2003; Passini 1984), whereas cognitive communications space constitutes a component of interpersonal communications among people. Thus, the elements of each cognitive entity are different. Cognitive space is dominated by physical elements, such as paths, landmarks, etc., while fellow people located in that cognized real space may or may not be part of such cognitive space. On the other hand, cognitive communications cyberspace is focused on the communicating parties, so that the surrounding physical environment, which may be viewed in video conversations, constitutes background only.

Cognitive communications space involves, however, several additional elements, beyond the direct physical surroundings of the calling parties, elements that pertain to human contacts. Foremost among these elements is language, which is essential for all communications, but it is even more so for online spoken or online written communications, in which, normally, the calling parties do not leave time for instant translation (something that is possible for the transmission of information in information space). The time framework is also essential if communications takes place in real time, and when the two parties are located in different domestic or international time zones. Such time differences apply not only to daily ones, but to weekend extents and holiday differences among nations, as well. These temporal differences between communicating parties may lead to time-space compression (see Chap. 5). Less crucial elements in communications cognitive space are weather conditions, which may potentially deter communications, and international currency differences, if merchandise and services are sold/bought internationally, during the conversation. Another element is the quality of communications, which is of much importance, notably for video conversations, and which may profit from broadband transmissions (see Chap. 4).

Cognitive real space and cognitive communications space differ also regarding some of their qualities as well as in their mapping. Cognitive space may yield cognitive maps in the minds of cognizing persons, and these maps may be externalized and drawn on paper. For the physical surroundings associated with video calls in cognitive communications space, such internal and external mappings seem irrelevant. Following Shum's (1990) distinction between locational and attributional information for traditional cognitive maps, we may claim that the cyberspace of interpersonal communications, as well as the cognitive cyberspace for such communications, include attributional information with no, or just a little, locational information. Furthermore, cognitive communications spaces are unique for each call and for each of the parties involved, and thus cannot be aggregated, whereas cognitive maps drawn by several people for a specific physical area may be compared, and conclusions on the wider knowledge of this area drawn. Cognitive real space and its cognitive mapping may facilitate *spatial behavior*, or corporeal personal mobility, whereas cognitive communications space may facilitate *social behavior*, in form of interpersonal communications. Furthermore, the cognition of real space may facilitate navigation or movement *in* places, whereas cognitive communications space may bring about bodily movement *to* other places for the sake of face-to-face meetings with the partners of Internet conversations, following successful virtual contacts (see Chap. 5 on proximity).

6.4 Conclusion

The discussions in this chapter have led us from the veteran notions of spatial cognition and cognitive maps, which were developed originally for real space, to the more novel cyberspatial Internet and its two classes of information and communications spaces, as potential producers of cognition and cognitive maps through the visual screen spaces employed by Internet users. Spatial cognition for real space may evolve out of a variety of internal and external sources, bringing about the development of cognitive or mental maps that can also be externalized on paper. The notion of personal space, referring to any personally experienced and cognized space, might also be relevant for cognitive cyberspaces.

Cognitive information space refers to the cognition of virtual spaces, mainly landscapes and maps, as viewed by Internet users. The very viewing of such spaces is partial, being restricted by screen sizes and currently available technologies for visual presentation. The rather partial cognition of virtual landscapes is further restricted by the probable inability of users to create mental maps following this cognition, given the partial sensual experience involved in the cognition of virtual landscapes. Thus, whereas for real space, space and its maps are two completely separated entities, in cyberspace they actually converge.

Cognitive communications space is even more complicated, as compared to cognitive information space. It refers to the cognition of real spaces that surround two communicating persons using video media, and these real spaces may only partially be sensed, experienced, or just imagined, over the contemporary variety of video communications media. These surrounding environments of the calling parties are perceived as belonging to the rather separate and unshared physical space of the parties. Cognitive communications space involves several additional elements, pertaining to human contacts: language, time of conversation, weather, quality of communications infrastructures, and international currency differences, in the case of business talks.

Internal and external mental mapping seem irrelevant for cognitive communications space. Cognitive communications space further differs from cognitive real space in that cognitive real space and its cognitive mapping may facilitate *spatial behavior*, whereas cognitive communications space may facilitate *social behavior*, in form of interpersonal communications. Furthermore, the cognition of real space may facilitate movement *in* places, whereas cognitive communications space may bring about bodily movement *to* other places for the sake of face-to-face meetings, following video conversations.

The increased use of electronic communications and its accompanying cognitive communications space constitute a major component of contemporary personal mobilities (Kellerman 2006, 2012). R&D (Research and development) within the information technology industry is still focused on innovations for the enhancement of such mobilities, so that the Internet information and communications spaces, and their accompanying cognitive spaces, may still change in the case of future introductions of new technologies.

References

Allen, J. (1999). Worlds within Cities. In D. Massey, J. Allen, & S. Pile (Eds.), *City Worlds* (pp. 53–97). London: Routledge.

Altman, I. (1975). *The Environment and Social Behavior: Privacy, Personal Space, Territory, Crowding*. Montrey, CA: Brooks/Cole.
Chang, Y.-L. (2003). Spatial cognition in digital cities. *International Journal of Architectural Computing, 1*, 471–488.
Dodge, M., & Kitchin, R. (2001). *Mapping Cyberspace*. London: Routledge.
Downs, R. M., & Stea, D. (1973). Cognitive maps and spatial behavior: Process and products. In R. M. Downs & D. Stea (Eds.), *Image and environment: Cognitive mapping and spatial behavior* (pp. 8–26). Chicago: Aldine.
Gale, N., & Golledge, R. (1982). On the subjective partitioning of space. *Annals of the Association of American Geographers, 72*, 60–67.
Golledge, R. G. (1995). Primitives of spatial knowledge. In T. L. Nyerges, D. M. Mark, R. Laurini, & M. J. Egehofer (Eds.), *Cognitive aspects of human-computer interaction for geographic information systems* (pp. 29–44). Boston: Kluwer.
Golledge, R.G. (1999). Human wayfinding and cognitive maps. In R.G. Golledge (Ed.), *Wayfinding behavior: Cognitive mapping and other spatial processes* (pp. 5–45). Baltimore: Johns Hopkins University Press.
Golledge, R. G., & Stimson, R. J. (1997). *Spatial behavior: A geographic perspective*. New York: Guilford Press.
Hochmair, H., & Frank, A. U. (2001). A semantic map as basis for the decision process in the WWW navigation. In D. R. Montello (Ed.), *Conference on spatial information theory* (pp. 173–188). Morrow Bay, CA: Springer.
Kellerman, A. (2006). *Personal mobilities*. London and New York: Routledge.
Kellerman, A. (2007). Cyberspace classification and cognition: Information and communications cyberspaces. *Journal of Urban Technology, 14*, 5–32.
Kellerman, A. (2012). *daily spatial mobilities: Physical and virtual*. Farnham and Burlington, VT: Ashgate.
Kitchin, R. (2001). Cognitive Maps. In N. J. Smelser & P. B. Bates (Eds.), *International encyclopedia of the social and behavioral sciences* (pp. 2120–2124). Oxford: Elsevier.
Kitchin, R., & Blades, M. (2002). *The cognition of geographic space*. New York: I.B.Tauris.
Kwan, M.-P. (2001). Cyberspatial cognition and individual access to information: The behavioral foundation of cybergeography. *Environment and planning B: Planning and design, 28*, 21–37.
Lynch, K. (1961). *The image of the city*. Cambridge, MA: MIT Press.
Passini, R. (1984). *Wayfinding in architecture*. New York: Van Nostrand Rheinhold.
Péruch, P., Gaunet, F., Thinus-Blanc, C., & Loomis, J. (2000). Understanding and learning virtual spaces. In R. Kitchin & S. Freundschuh (Eds.), *cognitive mapping: Past, present, and future* (pp. 108–124). London: Routledge.
Shields, R. (2003). *The virtual*. London and New York: Routledge.
Shum, S. (1990). Real and virtual spaces: Mapping from spatial cognition to hypertext. *Hypermedia, 2*, 133–158.
Sommer, R. (1969). *Personal space: The behavioral basis of design*. Englewood Cliffs, NJ: Prentice-Hall.
Tolman, E. C. (1948). Cognitive maps in rats and men. *Psychological Review, 55*, 189–208.

Chapter 7
Summary and Conclusion

Abstract This chapter will first present chapter summaries. This chapter will also discuss the geographic interpretations of the three Internet spaces in light of the geographical parameters presented in the previous chapters. It will then move to a concluding discussion which will focus on the possible combination between real and cyber spaces. By attempting to apply well-known concepts from traditional human geography to cyberspace, the book proposes, and if only a posteriori, some possible combination between these two geographies, a combination that may help in coping with Internet structures and contents.

Keywords Geographic parameters · Geographic interpretations · Spatial relations

This chapter will first present the chapter summaries for the six previous chapters. It will then move to a discussion of geographic interpretations for Internet spaces, focusing on the geographies of the three spaces of information, communications and screen, in light of the geographic parameters discussed in the previous chapters. The focus there on the Internet spaces will reverse the focus of the discussions, which so far has been on the parameters themselves. The concluding discussion in this chapter and for this book will attempt to explore possible combinations between real and cyber spaces, and will raise some thoughts for future studies.

7.1 Chapter Summaries

The Internet has been one of the fastest diffusing and adopted innovations, introduced originally in 1969, and maturing into an open code and universally available system, as of 1994. Some 22 years following its introduction, there are still global 'digital gaps' in the adoption of the system, internationally between developed and developing countries, as well as domestically within social sectors, such as age and gender. The international differences in the rates of Internet adoption between men and women depend on age group, culture and policy, and not necessarily on national

A. Kellerman, *Geographic Interpretations of the Internet*,
SpringerBriefs in Geography, DOI 10.1007/978-3-319-33804-0_7

economic development. The US dominates the registration and hosting of domains for websites, as well as in the transmission of information to and from them.

The social space of the Internet consists of several actors: users, computer and graphic website designers, and site owners. However, the Internet lacks the artistic, literal and philosophical descriptions and representations of space, which typify the attitudes towards real space. The numerous geographical dimensions that were proposed for the interpretation of the Internet demonstrate that it is, to a large degree, for users to shape their own personal cyberspatial geographies and cyberspatial experiences.

The terms and concepts that were discussed in the previous chapters are substantive, rather than methodological ones, and they were developed originally within several geographical epistemologies. The concepts introduced in Chap. 3 for the structure of Internet cyberspace were originally introduced and developed for real space by the regional approach, and they all relate to space *per se*. The concepts and terms introduced in Chap. 4 for distance in the Internet are mixed, in terms of their disciplinary origin and period of development, evolving either through the spatial-quantitative paradigm, or, as is the case for distanciation, as part of the sociological theory of structuration. Proximity, presented also in Chap. 4, jointly with almost all of the terms presented in Chap. 5 for mobility over the Internet, have been developed within the interdisciplinary study of mobilities, emerging as of the 1990s, and they all deal with dimensions of human individual behavior in space *vis-à-vis* spatial mobility. Finally, time-space compression discussed also in Chap. 5 refers again to individuals and was proposed within geography. The terminology for Chap. 6, notably for the study of spatial cognition and mental/cognitive mapping for real space, was developed mainly within behavioral geography, environmental psychology, and architecture.

In Chap. 2, we outlined the notion of 'space' as pertaining to the Internet. We presented image space as a mega-category consisting of four visual classes: virtual space, cyberspace, the Internet, and Internet screen spaces. We interpreted virtual space as the visual presentations of real space and real artifacts through both material and digital media, whereas cyberspace was viewed as referring to digital such presentations, notably through the Internet. As such, the Internet was suggested as constituting a subset of cyberspace, which on its part is a subset of the wider virtual space. Internet metaphorical space includes the two classes of information and communications spaces. This differentiation has led us to the presentation of the even more specific Internet screen-space as a third subset of the Internet.

Cyberspace has been spatially defined from the perspectives of artificial reality, interactivity, and conceptual and metaphorical spaces. Cyberspace was further shown to have a visual dimension through several media, including the Web and the communications platforms of the Internet. As a spatial experience, the exposure and use of cyberspace through the Internet involves co-presence in cyber and real space, low or nonexistent cognitive mapping ability of cyberspatial landscapes, and the facilitation of communication through, potentially at least, egalitarian and global platforms.

Chapters 3–5 explored three classes of geographical concepts developed for real space: structures, distance, and mobility. In Chap. 3 we explored the possible extension of the structuring, ordering and internal division of specific pieces of real space for interpretations of the cyberspatial Internet. We focused in this regard on the notions of ground or terrain, places, regions, and boundaries.

Screens may be viewed as being equivalent to physical ground. However, whereas real space consists of two layers, namely natural physical terrain and human-made space built on top of it, screen-space consists of a single human-made cyberspatial layer only, and thus it may be considered as ground *a posteriori* only. We may assess screens by their information density, similarly to measures of spatial density for population and for human-made artifacts in real space. Furthermore, screen information overloading may be viewed as being similar to information overloading for individuals experiencing dense and busy urban environments.

The 'ground' for Internet screens consists, specifically, of the graphic background that appears on screens for the presentation of information within it. Website designers take the equivalent role of both city planners and city governments in their design and creation of the background for information presented on screens. Users view information objects on screens from a vertical perspective, so that the design of website screens has to take into account the overall visuality of the screen. Sophisticated uses of visual and audial elements for screen background are of special significance and importance for commercial websites, notably in the tourism industry, attempting to create attractive and inviting virtual environments for their users.

Websites, or some of their specific pages, may potentially serve as virtual places in the Internet. The major difference between real space places and virtual ones is that the latter are not populated. However, the growing use of virtual places or Internet websites has turned users, at least in some restricted sense, into kind of residents that act and feel similarly to residents of real space places. Furthermore, the growing use of websites, at the expense of activities taking place in real space places, may weaken the forces, feelings, relations and performances attributed to the latter, in favor of the equivalent ones for virtual websites.

It is possible to apply to virtual places the four contemporary geographical interpretations proposed for real space places, all of which focus foremost on their residential population: First, there are capitalist forces that produce websites, followed by users-actors for the activities that take place in them (Neo-Marxist). Second, website users may experience place-related feelings under some circumstances (humanist). Third, access to websites and their use involve social relations, through societal sectoral gaps in levels of access to websites, as well as social relations involved in their use (feminist). Fourth, websites and networking platforms are typified by continuous change performance regarding the contents of websites (performative).

It is normally impossible to divide individual screens, perceived as ground, into regions of information presentation. In addition, the Web in general, which consists of millions of websites, is clearly unorganized along any systematic scalar or regional structures other than domain names. However, regions may be still identified both within websites and within the Web at large. Within websites, their size, measured by the number of screens, and the internal structure of websites, notably of portals, might be considered as a kind of regional subdivision, with 'regional' in this case, not carrying a geographical connotation. The Web system in general is divided along the two suffixes of the URL domain addresses, namely by information or organization type of domain owners, and by the country of domain registration. Both classifications exhibit heavy American dominance in the production side of Internet information.

International boundaries in physical space still have some significance for the overall patterns of interpersonal communications over the Internet, with individuals preferring to communicate with fellows located close by in real space. Interpersonal communications might be sanctioned by cultural and religious norms, as well as by governmental censorships preventing or controlling international communications. Websites are normally open for full or partial free use by domestic as well as by international users, and they are interconnected with each other through links that are proposed on their pages. Such links may direct users to websites from all over the world. Thus, information may flow freely across international borders where permitted, as compared to the flows of people and commodities which are still controlled by all countries or unions of countries, such as the EU.

In Chap. 4, we examined the status and significance of distance in general, as well as its derivatives of distance decay, distanciation, and proximity, all of them for their possible application for the interpretation of the Internet *per se*, i.e. mainly within cyberspace itself. Distance, as a measure of separation, may be applied to the cyberspatial Internet by the number of clicks required either for the reaching of a specific piece of information, for the reaching of a website, or for the reaching of specific people, in order to communicate with them.

Distance decay has been recognized as a basic pattern for spatial organization in real space. We presented distance decay patterns also for the two Internet classes of information and communications spaces. There are two patterns of distance decay for the Internet information space. In surfing to specific websites, access duration increases with growing physical distance between calling users and called hosting servers. These hosting servers constitute centers, and their users are located around them by increasing physical distance and accompanying growing access time, measured by latency through pings. In website searches via search engines, the order of search results, presented on Internet screens, is of special significance, since users prefer to access the first result, which serves, therefore, as a center on the Internet screen, with declining uses of lower ranked results. In the Internet communications space, communications and networking permit contacts among Internet users without regard of their distances from each other. Still, in practice, users, as centers, keep more ties with people located physically closer to them.

Generally, then, distance decay in the Internet presents diversified appearances, with hosting servers (for surfing), screen locations (for searching), and users' physical locations (for networking) as centers, and with varying decay measurements, respectively: time (for surfing), on screen distance of presentation (for searches), and physical distance (for communications).

Distanciation refers to the increasing geographical spread of potential destinations for human actions at large. Distanciation can be measured specifically for individual uses of the Internet, through the spatial extent of consulted websites by users, as well as through the location of their contacted professional colleagues and social friends. The destinations for these informational and interpersonal activities can be domestic only, or they can be foreign ones as well, potentially reaching a globalization of the spread of Internet sources accessed by specific users.

Proximity, or nearness, among communicating people, may develop in a rather stratified manner along numerous Internet communications levels, facilitated by the availability of written, audial and video communications platforms. Such a stratification of communications may fit, for example, evolving romantic or business relationships, which may go up along the whole or part of the communications ladder using changing virtual communications media, so that only if virtual communications proves satisfactory, then face-to-face contacting may be called for.

In Chap. 5, we focused on elements of mobility and their operations in cyberspace, thus exploring terms that have been proposed within the study of mobilities, notably those related to personal mobilities. We presented, first, the notion of cyber-mobility, referring to the very mobility of people through the Internet, followed by discussions of six specific mobility notions: flow, speed, directionality, circularity, co-presence, and time-space compression.

Cyber-mobility constitutes the mobility of information, of all types and for all purposes, through the cyberspatial Internet. Cyber-mobility has become increasingly significant along the gradual introduction of technological innovations, which have permitted faster information transmissions, culminating with mobile broadband for smartphones. Thus, personal mobilities about cities may involve simultaneously real and virtual mobilities, implying a decreasing experiencing of urban landscapes, when walking or driving through cities.

Flows of information were considered being as flexible as the movements of gas, and flows within the Internet were viewed like fluids of social relations, with varying degrees of freedom of movements, depending on the type of networks. Flows for individuals in cyberspatial contexts refer to the flows of information along screen sequences, as well as to the flows of the interactions of users with websites, notably with service oriented ones. Flows can, thus, be measured by the rate of unsuccessful completions of transactions per session of website use, and/or by the time it takes for the completion of successful ones.

The contemporary urgencies for immediacy and instantaneity in life pace in general, have led to the growing rush for the production and consumption of increasing fixed and mobile broadband Internet speeds, mainly in developed countries. These faster speeds have permitted the turning of the Internet into service and entertainment action spaces, on the demand side, side by side with their constitution of production landscapes for business, on the supply side. Broadband speed availabilities differ among countries, as well as among specific places and given times of use. Information transmission speeds over the Internet can be measured through the ping utility.

Directionality, or predefined geographical destinations for specific movements, typifies most movements in physical space, but this is mostly not the case for cyberspatial movements. In the communications space of the Internet, messages are geared for people as destinations, and message addressees may retrieve them through mobile communications devices, while being located anywhere in real space. Similarly, in both information searches and in surfing to specific websites, users are interested in the contents and the identity of the consulted websites, but not in the changing geographical locations in physical space of the servers that host them. Generally then, cyberspatial directionality refers to Internet destinations, namely people in the communications space, and websites or information, in the information space. The real space locations for these destinations, namely their hosting servers, seem irrelevant for their users in most cases. It is still possible, though, to trace the location of these servers through some specific tracing tools.

Circularity of movements constitutes the usual case for Internet users, who may begin their surfing or search sessions at their homepage, and returning normally there at the end of their use sessions. However, Internet surfing sessions may not just reach a single destination, but they may involve surfing to numerous websites in sequence. In addition, some Internet use sessions may frequently be cyclical, for instance, when the same website is being used periodically. Both the circularity and the cyclicality of Internet use sessions can be simply measured by noting the specific websites from which surfing begins, the websites visited during any session, and the website in which sessions conclude.

We paid detailed attention to co-presence, or the simultaneous presence of Internet users in both real and virtual spaces, given its being a basic experience occurring for all the uses of the Internet. We have noted a wide variety of co-presence scenarios, emerging when individuals reach out, through the Internet, to all five possible types of attractions or communications stimuli: fellow people, places, events, information, and things. Co-presence is obviously also the case when individuals are engaged in reaching out to combinations among these attractions, notably within urban contexts. Reaching out virtually through co-presence involves particular functions and patterns attributed to each of the attractions, and these may bring about the very reaching out of Internet users to them. Mobile phones, tablets and laptops, permit people's engagement in location-free extensive virtual co-presences.

We further noted the wide assessment by relevant studies of virtual co-presence of its being an inferior experience, notably for interpersonal interactions, as compared to those attained in real space only. Still, it is important to note that the contemporary information age has provided for an impressive array of opportunities for co-presences, facilitated by communications technologies that permit personal mobility, through the continuous availability of these personal communications devices. Thus, contemporary individuals in the developed world experience co-presence much more extensively than they did just a decade or two ago, but these virtual co-presence experiences might amount to shallower experiences, as compared to face-to-face ones in real space. Even under the circumstances of growing mobile communications, cities have kept their feature as foci for co-presences, but these co-presences include now simultaneous face-to-face and virtual ones, in public as well as in private urban spheres.

Time-space compression may emerge in global social interactions by individuals, as well as in domestic and global, and thus continuous, work-related interactions experienced by workers. The degree of time-space compression of Internet users may be easily measured through the timings of their communications sessions.

The discussions in Chap. 6 have led us from the veteran notions of spatial cognition and cognitive maps, which were developed originally for real space, to the more novel cyberspatial Internet and its two classes of information and communications spaces, as potential producers of cognition and cognitive maps among their users. Spatial cognition for real space may evolve out of a variety of internal and external sources, bringing about the development of cognitive or mental maps that can also be externalized on paper.

Cognitive information space refers to the cognition of virtual spaces, mainly landscapes and maps, as viewed by Internet users. The very viewing of such spaces is partial, being restricted by screen sizes and the currently available technologies for visual presentation. The rather partial cognition of virtual landscapes is further restricted by the probable inability of users to create mental maps following this cognition, given the partial sensual experience involved in the cognition of virtual landscapes. Thus, whereas for real space, space and its maps are two completely separated entities, in cyberspace they actually converge. However, the notion of personal space, as referring to any personally experienced and cognized space, might also be relevant for cognitive cyberspaces.

Cognitive communications space presents scenarios that are even more complicated than those mentioned for cognitive information space. Cognitive communications space refers to the cognition of real spaces that surround two communicating persons during their use of video media, and these real spaces may be partially sensed, experienced, or just imagined, over the contemporary variety of video communications media. However, these surrounding environments of the calling parties are perceived as belonging to the rather separate and unshared physical space of the parties. Cognitive communications space involves several additional elements, pertaining to human contacts: language, time of conversation, weather, quality of communications infrastructures, and international currency differences, in the case of business talks.

Internal and external mental mapping by Internet users seem irrelevant for cognitive communications space. Cognitive communications space further differs from cognitive real space in that cognitive real space and its cognitive mapping may facilitate *spatial behavior*, whereas cognitive communications space may facilitate *social behavior*, in form of interpersonal communications. Furthermore, the cognition of real space may facilitate movement *in* places, whereas cognitive communications space may bring about bodily movement *to* other places for the sake of face-to-face meetings following successful virtual communications.

The increased use of electronic communications and its accompanying cognitive communications space constitute a major component of contemporary personal mobilities (Kellerman 2006, 2012). R&D (Research and development) within the information technology industry is still focused on innovations for the enhancement of virtual personal mobilities, so that cyberspace classes, and their accompanying cognitive spaces, may still change in case of future introduction of new technologies.

7.2 Geographic Interpretations for Internet Spaces

Our discussions in Chaps. 3–6 focused on 15 parameters originally developed for the study of real space geography, aiming at examinations of their possible relevance for a geographical interpretation of the Internet and its spaces, as well. Table 7.1 summarizes these discussions by presenting all the 15 parameters along its lines. In addition, the table permits, by looking at its four columns, to reverse our perspective. We can examine now the three Internet spaces of information, communications, and screens from a geographical perspective, thus noting which geographical parameters are relevant for each Internet space, what is the geography of each Internet space all about, and what are the measures for the relevant parameters. These latter measures for the parameters are highly varied, being quantitative for some of the parameters, and qualitative for others. We will now briefly examine the geographical parameters pertaining to each Internet space/table column.

7.2.1 Geographic Parameters for the Interpretation of Internet Information Space

As it turns out, the Internet information space can be interpreted in light of numerous geographical parameters, thus presenting a profile of a space, even if only a metaphorical one, that may be interpreted through geographical parameters. The Web is divided, through the suffixes of website URL addresses, into non-geographical regions by the suffix relating to the type of contents or the type of website owners. The Web is further divided into kind of geographical regions by yet another suffix, that which presents the country of domain registration. Users enjoy a potential global reach for websites, possibly restricted by international boundaries in real space, which may bring about some governmental censorship on international reach. The use of the Web, or the Internet information space, involves the simultaneous co-presence of users in real space and in virtual space for any of the chosen use attractions: information, places, events or things. Web screens, notably those presenting landscapes, may be partially cognized as personal spaces, but without the resulting development of cognitive maps. The very use of particular websites, notably those that are about places or that are structured like them, involves some place experiencing for the users.

Website access implies some latency, which increases with growing distance between users and website hosting servers. This latency might be significant for the transmission of large data sets over long distances. The required time for website use and the convenience of its use depends on the efficiency of screen sequences, or their flows. Moving from one website to other ones, or distances within the system, requires the operation of clicks, the number of which presents distances within the system. Reaching the desired attraction (information, places, events or things)

Table 7.1 Parameters for geographic interpretations of Internet spaces and their measures

Internet spaces and measures	Internet information space	Internet communications space	Internet screen space	Parameter measures
Parameters				
Ground			Background as ground	Information density; background attractiveness
Place	Websites experienced as places			Neo-Marxist; humanist; feminist; performative
Regions	Web and website divisions			Website size; domain addresses
Boundaries	International boundaries as barriers	International boundaries as barriers		Cultural and national censorships
Distance	Linking to other pages	Linking to other possible contacts		Number of clicks
Distance decay	Website access latency growing with distance from servers	Declining contacts with growing distance in real space	Preference for the top results on the first screen of search results	Ping utility for latency; distances for communications; presentation order for screens
Distanciation	Potential global reach	Potential global reach		Actual spatial extent of reach
Proximity		Stratified proximity through preferred media		Choice of communications medium per call
Flow	Screen sequences			Rate of success and duration per website use
Speed	Transmissions of information	Video call quality		Ping utility
Directionality	Information as destination	People as destinations		Server tracing tools
Circularity	Return to homepage at the end of sessions			Website at which sessions terminate
Co-presence	Simultaneous presence in real and virtual spaces	Simultaneous presence in real and virtual spaces		
Time-space compression		Long-distance online interactions		Timing of communications
Cognition	Partial cognition but no cognitive mapping	Partial cognition but no cognitive mapping		

consists destination for users, regardless of the physical location of website hosting servers. Users perform circular sessions, in that they normally begin and conclude their use session at the homepages of their computers.

Out of the fifteen geographical parameters proposed for the geographical interpretation of the Internet, four ones apply exclusively for the interpretation of information space: perception and experiencing of websites as places; the division of the Web and websites into regions; the flow sequences of website screens, and the return of users to their homepages at the end of use sessions.

7.2.2 Geographic Parameters for the Interpretation of Internet Communications Space

Communications of Internet users with fellow users through the varied contacting options offered by the Internet communications space has its own geography, as well. Some of the parameters for this geography are unique for this space, and the potential richness of its geographical interpretation is somehow lower, as compared to information space.

Like the exposures to any other virtual attraction, which we noted in the previous subsection, exposure to fellow people through Internet communications, notably online, always involves co-presence of users in both real and virtual spaces. Contacting people online at long-distances, notably when requiring late night communications, may imply also time-space compression for users. Subscribers of Internet communications may potentially contact people globally, as long as there are no censorships and other political barriers stemming from international boundaries in real space for such contacts. However, preference is given by callers to the calling of people located close by in real space. Communicating individuals view contacted fellows as their virtual destinations, with the virtual distances that separate among them measured by the number of clicks required for reaching them. Contacting with others may constitute a rather stratified process, using preferred communications media that fit the type and phase of the social relations between the communicating parties. The availability of fast broadband connection may facilitate or enhance video calls, in which the spatial background surrounding the called person and viewed on the screen, possibly cognized as personal space, but without resulting cognitive mapping.

Out of the fifteen geographical parameters proposed for the geographical interpretation of the Internet, just two ones apply exclusively for the interpretation of communications space: stratified proximity between callers through preferred uses of communications media, and time-space compression in cases of long-distance online communications.

Some of the geographical parameters for the cyberspatial Internet, in both of its spaces, are anchored in some way in real space. Thus, the very use of the system involves co-presence in both real and virtual spaces. Furthermore, the system permits global reach, but international boundaries in physical space may have an impact on the extent of reach. Even when there are no barriers for information transmissions and interpersonal communications, growing distances between users and website hosting servers in real space may bring about some latency, and growing distances between users and their social contacts in physical space may normally imply declining social relations.

7.2.3 Geographic Parameters for the Interpretation of Internet Screen Space

The geographical interpretation of Internet screen spaces consists of a small number of parameters, so that its geographical interpretation is more limited, as compared to the two other Internet spaces. Internet screens, and notably in their being a background for information presentation, may be considered like ground in real space, potentially providing for use convenience and attractiveness. The ordering of screen presentations has a special significance for result pages of searches performed through search engines. The order of the results presents distance decay from the result appearing on top of the first result page downwards, in terms of levels of attraction and use by searchers. This distance decay pattern on search result screens turns the presented results into locations, and the first result into a center. Location, a most basic geographical parameter, is irrelevant for the rather virtual Internet information and communications spaces, but it turns out to be of crucial importance on the visual Internet screen spaces.

7.2.4 Geographic Interpretations of the Internet

Following our separate discussions of each of the three Internet information spaces, let us now look at a geographic interpretation of the Internet system in general. In total, we have noticed some four parameters that apply exclusively to information space, two parameters that apply exclusively for communications space, and just a single parameter that applies exclusively to Internet screen space. Thus, some eight parameters, or over one-half of the total number of parameters, apply to the geographical interpretation of both information and communications spaces, and they present a kind of a general profile for geographic features of Internet cyberspace at large, as follows.

The use of the Internet for all contacts, including people, events, places, information and things, implies the immersion of users in co-presence, in real and virtual spaces. However, the viewed spaces on Internet screens may only partially be cognized, and this cognition does not lead to the development of cognitive maps.

The Internet facilitates a potential global reach or access to both information (websites) and people. Thus, Internet users are focused on the reaching of desired information and people, and not in the terrestrial location of the contacted servers and computers, respectively. However, this utmost global potential reach for Internet spaces is bound by the preference of users to contact people who are located close to them in real space, as well as by some latency in the transmission of large data sets from and to servers located remotely. Another geographically limiting factor, applying to a significant share of Internet users, are international boundaries in real space, which may affect the geography of their reach of information and/or people, given the impositions of governmental censorships by some countries. Despite the lack of physical distances within cyberspace, distances within and among websites still exist, expressed by the number of clicks users need to make for moving from one specific page, or cyberspatial location, to other pages and to linked websites, as well as to contacted people. The high speeds of operation that typify the system provide for a rather efficient movement within websites, thus requiring a proper organization of screen sequences by website owners.

The cyberspatial Internet is intertwined with real space. We will discuss in the next session some specific relations between the two spaces. However, we can point now, at the conclusion of the discussion on the geographical parameters for Internet interpretation, to some dependencies of the Internet on real space. Real space is where users live, thus requiring co-presence with cyberspace; it is in real space where internet users maintain their social face-to-face relations; it is in real space where Internet hardware is located; and, finally, it is in real space in which countries enforce their national boundaries on cyberspace.

The geography of the cyberspatial Internet *per se* is composed of several circles, contained within each other (Fig. 7.1; see also Fig. 2.1). The widest one stands for

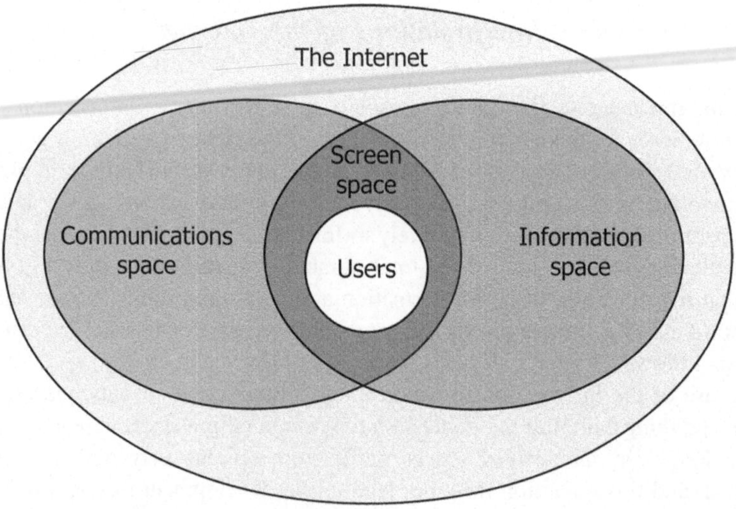

Fig. 7.1 The Internet and its spaces

the Internet as a system with the following features that we noted already: it requires co-presence; it is based on the speed of light; it facilitates potential global reach of people and information; it enables the reach of information and people without regard of their real space locations; and it is based on clicks as a separating effect, similarly to real space distance. Within this wider circle, there are two additional equal ones, those of information and communications spaces. These two Internet spaces partially overlap each other and in two ways. First, it is possible to communicate with website owners through their websites, and it is possible to send information files through e-mail and chats, as well as link e-mails with specific websites. Second, Internet screens serve both spaces as their visual interfaces with users.

Internet information space and its websites present several specific geographical features: they may be perceived as places; they may be divided into region-like parts; their screen sequences present flows; and circularity may be attributed to the return of users to their homepages at the end of use sessions. Two geographical features are associated with the Internet communications space: callers may enjoy stratified proximity between them through preferred uses of communications media, and time-space compression may be experienced in cases of long-distance online communications.

As we mentioned already, screens serve the Internet spaces of information and communications, constituting the visual interface with their users. Screens constitute, therefore, an inner circle of the Internet. They constitute the equivalent of ground in real space, with information presented on them being similar to human-made artifacts in real space. Internet users are at the center of the set of geographical circles for the Internet described so far. Their specific personal patterns of Internet uses for the consultation of information and for the contacting of people produce and present their own personal cyberspatial geographies, for instance in terms of the extent of their geographical reach, their possible application of circular use patterns, and their preferred uses via fixed and/or mobile devices.

7.3 Relations Between Real and Cyber Spaces

In an attempt to apply well-known concepts from traditional human geography to cyberspace, the book proposed some possible transcendence of terminology for the geographical interpretation of space from real space to cyberspace. This transcendence points to some possible combination between terrestrial and virtual geographies, and such a combination may help in coping with Internet structures and contents. We have attempted to demonstrate that it is possible to extend several of the basic notions pertaining to the structuring, distancing and movement in real space for the understanding of cyberspace via the Internet and its components, and in numerous ways. We believe that jointly, the discussions of the15 parameters for the geographical interpretation of Internet spaces may propose at least a beginning for a systematic geography of the Internet and its components.

The differences between real and virtual spaces have been portrayed and discussed elsewhere (see e.g. Kellerman 2014), and some of the relationships between virtual space and physical (absolute and relative) spaces were elaborated by Wang et al. (2003). Despite its seemingly illusive and metaphorical nature, cyberspace may be considered as an ontic entity involving geographical experiencing by its users via the Internet. However, the geographical nature of this experiencing differs from that of real space in numerous ways. First, cyberspace experiencing is normally much more extensive in its spatial extent as compared to that of real space, with users possibly contacting websites and people located far away from their location in real space. Second, cyberspace use may be temporally much more intensive than travels in real space, given the possibility for extended use sessions. Third, and in contrary to the first two points, we noted in the previous chapter that cyberspace experiencing seems to be shallower than that of real space in its perceptional imprint on users. Finally and fourth, cyberspace experiencing lacks almost any bodily involvement by its users, and this lack of bodily involvement may contribute to the lower experiential imprint on its users.

The omnipresence of the Internet and its instant accessibility have amounted to a practical, rather than theoretical, integration of physical and virtual spaces for users. The instant access of users to broadband services has brought about some implications for contemporary society, which is typified by the generally wider availability and use of communications media. First, growing virtual mobility may increase rather than decrease physical mobility, since one does not have to be tied to a desktop any more in order to instantly initiate, receive and respond to digital messages, including long international telephone calls, which may be performed via free or low cost VoIP services. Second, the speeding up of daily activities, whether for economic production or for social communications, may reach now a higher level, since all communications and information media have become fully mobile, thus prompting continuous attention by users to incoming messages in their mobile communications devices. Third, the blurring of the separation between work/business and leisure which has typified the spheres of work and home in recent years, will intensify, since work and social activities can now be easily performed when away from both office and home. This blurring between work and leisure amounts also to the blurring between real and virtual spaces. A similar point, relating to social relationships, was made by Licoppe (2004), who recognized an emerging pattern of continuous 'connected relationships' through a variety of media of electronic communications, so that 'the boundaries between absence and presence eventually get blurred' (p. 136).

7.4 Future Study

A possible future accumulation of empirical findings from studies that will apply some of the numerous measures and dimensions proposed for the geographical analysis of the Internet, may bring about a better understanding of cyberspace uses, notably as compared to real space ones. It may further lead to a classification of both websites and Internet user sessions into categories, based on website features, and on patterns of their usage, respectively. Beyond the research arena, the proposed parameters for a geographical interpretation of the Internet may serve as a teaching aid for the geographical study of cyberspace and the Internet, as categories of human-made space, side by side with the more traditional geographical study of human-made real space.

As demonstrated in the previous chapters, there are altogether some fifteen parameters which have been originally developed and used for the analysis of human-made real space, and which can be applied to the geographical interpretation of the Internet, as well. Some of these parameters concern spatial aspects of the Internet system from the perspective of users, whereas others relate to spatial aspects for the very operation and structure of the system, whereas some additional parameters refer to socio-spatial aspects of the Internet, mainly those pertaining to social networking or communications. Thus, it is possible to analyze some qualities of a given website or portal from their users' perspective, using geographical tools, separately or jointly with a geographical analysis of several aspects concerning the operational structure and organization of that website or portal. In addition, the very use of the Internet by its subscribers has to be assessed also per use session, since several of the use parameters may change from session to session. For instance, the speed of transmission may be measured by the broadband speeds assured by the ISP, which are usually fixed, but the specific speed of transmission per transaction, or 'per screen', may change at any given time of operation.

References

Kellerman, A. (2006). *Personal Mobilities*. London and New York: Routledge.

Kellerman, A. (2012). *Daily Spatial Mobilities: Physical and Virtual*. Farnham and Burlington, VT: Ashgate.

Kellerman, A. (2014). *The Internet as Second Action Space*. London and New York: Routledge.

Licoppe, C. (2004). 'Connected' presence: The emergence of a new repertoire for managing social relationships in a changing communication technoscape. *Environment and Planning D: Society and Space., 22*, 135–156.

Wang, Y., Lai, P., & Sui, D. (2003). Mapping the Internet using GIS: The death of distance hypothesis revisited. *Journal of Geographical Systems, 5*, 381–405.